TICKLE ME SILLY, GOD

AN INVITATION TO EXPERIENCE

THE JOY OF THE LORD

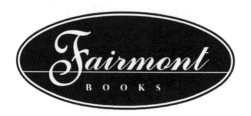

Fairmont

BOOKS

KIM KRAEMER

Tickle Me Silly, God
Copyright © 1999 by Kim Kraemer
ALL RIGHTS RESERVED

Fairmont Books is a ministry of The McDougal Foundation, Inc., a Maryland nonprofit corporation dedicated to spreading the Gospel of the Lord Jesus Christ to as many people as possible in the shortest time possible.

Published by:

Fairmont Books
P.O. Box 3595
Hagerstown, MD 21742-3595
www.mcdougal.org

ISBN 1-884369-98-7

Printed in the United States of America
For Worldwide Distribution

DEDICATION

I would like to dedicate this book to you, the reader, who, having read and digested its contents, will multiply in the Earth, running the race effectively for the joy set before you. God speed, O child of God. May His joy unspeakable flow in and out of you for His glory revealed in the Earth.

Amen and Amen!

ACKNOWLEDGMENTS

I have many people to thank:

Bishop Bill and Evelyn Hamon of Christian International, who provided me with covering, oversight and friendship and who continue to pioneer the apostolic and prophetic move of God.

All my mentors whom I have had the honor to serve.

My beloved husband Ron, for his continual labor of love with me in this ministry.

My beloved children, B.J. and Heather, who have brought great joy to my life.

My mom, Beulah Oldham, who taught me never to give up on my dreams and who faithfully nurtured and trained up her children, showing us, by her example, a servant's heart.

My dearest friend, Sue Farmer, who painstakingly transcribed this material from tape.

My faithful prayer warrior at The 700 Club, who prayed through with me so that I could begin this ministry of joy.

My faithful partner in prayer, Rosia Carter, who, as I talked about writing the book, said, "Just do it, Kim."

Harold McDougal, who diligently worked with me on this book so that it could go forth into all the Earth.

The wilderness and the solitary place shall BE GLAD for them; and the desert shall rejoice, and blossom as the rose. It shall blossom abundantly, and REJOICE EVEN WITH JOY AND SINGING: the glory of Lebanon shall be given unto it, the excellency of Carmel and Sharon, they shall see the glory of the Lord, and the excellency of our God. Strengthen ye the weak hands, and confirm the feeble knees. Say to them that are of a fearful heart, Be strong, fear not: behold, your God will come with vengeance, even God with a recompence; He will come and save you.

Then the eyes of the blind shall be opened, and the ears of the deaf shall be unstopped. Then shall the lame man leap as an hart, and the tongue of the dumb sing: for in the wilderness shall waters break out, and streams in the desert. And the parched ground shall become a pool, and the thirsty land springs of water: in the habitation of dragons, where each lay, shall be grass with reeds and rushes. And an highway shall be there, and a way, and it shall be called The way of holiness; the unclean shall not pass over it; but it shall be for those: the wayfaring men, though fools, shall not err therein. No lion shall be there, nor any ravenous beast shall go up thereon, it shall not be found there; but the redeemed shall walk there: And the ransomed of the Lord shall return, and COME TO ZION WITH SONGS AND EVERLASTING JOY UPON THEIR HEADS: THEY SHALL OBTAIN JOY AND GLADNESS, AND SORROW AND SIGHING SHALL FLEE AWAY.　　　　　　　　　　Isaiah 35:1-10

CONTENTS

Foreword by Ruth Ward Heflin 9

Foreword by Dr. Rochelle Miller 10

Foreword by Nancy Graham 11

Introduction 13

Part I: The Biblical Basis for Laughter 15

  1. Why God Laughs 17

  2. Why Believers Laugh 34

  3. Why Unbelievers Laugh 43

  4. What Is False Laughter? 59

  5. When I Began to Laugh in the Spirit 63

Part II: Laughter and the Fruits of the Spirit 73

  6. Love and Laughter 75

  7. Joy and Laughter 81

  8. Peace and Laughter 87

  9. Longsuffering [Patience] and Laughter 92

10. Faith [Faithfulness] and Laughter 95

11. Meekness [Humility] and Laughter 98

12. Temperance [Self-control] and Laughter 104

13. Protecting the Fruits of the Spirit in Your
     Life 110

**Part III: Keeping Godly Laughter Working in
Your Life** 117

14. The Joy Robbers 119
15. A Time to Weep 131
16. Tickle Me Silly, God 134

My Prayer for You 139

About the Author 143
Ministry Address 144

FOREWORD BY
RUTH WARD HEFLIN

Kim Kraemer's revelation of the importance of the ministry of joy and laughter in this last-day revival is a great key to being able to maintain and sustain revival. The knowledge that *"the joy of the Lord is my strength"* is not human knowledge, but revelation knowledge, and becomes revelation experience to the yielded vessel through the manifestation of holy laughter. In this regard, *Tickle Me Silly, God,* is a timely gift to the Body of Christ.

Ruth Ward Heflin
Ashland, Virginia

FOREWORD BY
DR. ROCHELLE MILLER

Kim Kraemer is a wonderful gift to the Body of Christ. As you read this book, it becomes quite evident that she is not merely talking of a "concept," but personal knowledge and understanding that only comes from experiencing the wonderful joy of the Lord.

Kim is an energetic and faith-filled woman of God and is a joy to be around. She is positively contagious! She has nailed it in these few simple words, "Holy joy is oil on the wheels of our Christian experience."

Tickle Me Silly, God is truly a God-breathed word, and I encourage you to prayerfully read it and allow the Holy Spirit to touch you, rearrange some of your thinking and fill you with His joy!

Dr. Rochelle Miller, Founder
His Glory To See Ministries & Dunamis Cafe
Charleston, West Virginia

FOREWORD BY
NANCY GRAHAM

Kim Kraemer is a special friend and encourager, a mighty warrior with a gusto passion to serve God and make Him known. How appropriate that God has chosen this anointed vessel to write *Tickle Me Silly, God*, a liberating truth in a timely season, to call to our remembrance that *"the joy of the Lord is our strength."* Jesus had more joy than any other man, and He intended that we be His joyful representatives in the Earth.

Enjoy and rejoice as you discover a passionate, life-changing, yet distinctly believers way of success, ignited by the joy of the Lord.

Thank you, Kim, for being obedient to the Holy Spirit.

Nancy Graham
Missionary-Evangelist
New Life World Outreach

INTRODUCTION

I was blessed very early in my Christian experience to receive a revelation of how very important joy and laughter is to the believer. If we are to maintain the freshness of our experience, if we are to be sustained in an intimate walk with the Father, somehow we must gain release from the pressures of daily life, and laughter does this for us.

So many things are pulling on us at the same time, and we sometimes don't realize the cumulative effect this constant pressure has on our spirits. People, things and the world are pulling on us. Even brothers and sisters in the Lord are pulling on us. We need to experience the release that comes with the joy of the Lord. We need to laugh, sometimes until we get downright silly. Laughter sets us free, and there is something wonderfully liberating about getting tickled silly for the Lord Jesus Christ. It not only releases us, it strengthens us; and it is a powerful weapon for spiritual warfare.

If you had a brother or sister who tickled you when you were a child, you may understand what I am talking about. They sometimes tickled us until we felt silly, and it was somehow a wonderfully exhilarating feeling. Afterward we felt ready for anything.

Receiving the overflowing joy of the Lord, being tickled silly by God, is different in one important way from our experience as children. This joy begins on the inside and is not a response to any outside stimuli. It has, however, that same wonderful exhilarating effect and leaves us giddy with joy and ready to tackle the world.

This is not a fleshly experience. It is truly from God. As proof, God is sending joyful waves of laughter into the lives of believers all over the world, especially where revival is being experienced. Many who are laughing in the Spirit have never heard of this experience or read about its appearance in revivals of former times. It is spontaneous and life-changing. It is time that we get past the negative mindset that many in the Body of Christ have concerning laughter.

God has given me a ministry of joy, and I have been very blessed over the past years to be able to carry the good news of His gift of joy to many parts of the world. Now, for the first time, I want to share this message with more of God's wonderful people in many countries through the vehicle of this book. May God bless you as you read it, and may you be filled with joy and laughter in the Holy Ghost. For in His presence IS fullness of joy.

Kim Kraemer
JMI

PART I

THE BIBLICAL BASIS FOR LAUGHTER

ONE

WHY GOD LAUGHS

He that sitteth in the heavens shall laugh.
                                                Psalm 2:4

Many have not yet realized that our God is a God of laughter. Maybe we have just never thought about it. Where did laughter originate? Clearly, God is the author of laughter. It came from Him.

In the case of Psalm 2, God was laughing at His enemies. He does that often. The rest of the passage declares:

> *Why do the heathen rage, and the people imagine a vain thing?*
> *The kings of the earth set themselves, and the*

rulers take counsel together, against the LORD,
and against His anointed, saying,
Let us break their bands asunder, and cast away
their cords from us.
He that sitteth in the heavens shall laugh: the
Lord shall have them in derision.

Psalm 2:1-4

Many Bible verses show us how tickled God gets with men and their constant scheming. God is confident, and when men threaten Him, He just laughs.

How presumptuous of men to threaten the Almighty! It is laughable when you stop to think about it. No wonder God laughs! He has every right to do it.

Many times our narrow-mindedness prevents us from understanding the greatness and the power of God, and we worry and fret about many things and about many people. While we are worrying ourselves to death, God is laughing. As the Scriptures declare:

If God be for us, who can be against us?

Romans 8:31

Nothing men can do threatens Him in any way. He knows the frailty of men, and He certainly knows His own strength. His strength has no limits. All the heathen put together cannot possibly stand against the might of our God. That's why He laughs. He continues to laugh, even when *"all the heathen"* unite against Him:

> *But Thou, O LORD, shalt laugh at them; Thou shalt have all the heathen in derision.*
>
> Psalm 59:8

No wonder God laughs! He is right to laugh.

Please don't misunderstand me. God is not laughing at the tragedies that befall men. In fact, He is not really laughing at men at all. He is laughing at the power behind the men. He is laughing at the forces that make men act like they do. He is laughing at evil. He has said:

> *For we wrestle not against flesh and blood, but against principalities, against powers, against the rulers of the darkness of this world, against spiritual wickedness in high places.*
>
> Ephesians 6:12

Learning this truth can help us to love those around us. We know that God's Word instructs us to love all men, even our enemies, but it is not always an easy thing to do. If we can understand that those who persecute us are motivated by evil spirits, it makes it so much easier to love them.

If we want to get angry with someone, we should get angry with the devil. We should not be turned off by the mocking attitude of people. We should not allow the haughtiness that men display disturb our spirits. We should love them anyhow, for God is love. We need to be quick in yielding ourselves to the ministry of the Holy Spirit and allow God's love to flow through us, for He promised:

> *He that believeth on Me, as the Scripture hath said, out of his belly shall flow rivers of living water.* John 7:38

Most people don't even realize how badly they are acting. They are yielded to wicked spirits and are being motivated by unseen forces. When men and women are still in darkness, what can we expect of them? Until they have been delivered from the kingdom of darkness there is little hope that they will act properly. Just love them anyway.

We are representatives of God and must show forth His love to the world around us. It is in this way that we will win men to His Kingdom. God just laughs at the enemy, and we must learn to laugh at him too.

This is confirmed strongly in the Scriptures when we see that God not only laughs when enemies rise against Him, He also laughs when enemies rise against His children:

> *The wicked plotteth against the just, and gnasheth upon him with his teeth. The Lord shall laugh at him: for He seeth that his day is coming.* Psalm 37:12-13

How presumptuous of men to oppose God's children! How foolish! God laughs when it happens, and we should learn to laugh too.

If God can laugh when everyone and everything seem to turn against us, so can we. We can laugh in the face of the enemy. Yes, right in his face. We can laugh in the face of adversity. We can laugh in difficult circumstances. We can laugh because God laughs. When Father laughs, we can laugh, too.

We focus far too much on the problems we are facing at the moment, on the devil and on his opposition to us. When we do this our problems become so great in our eyes that it seems as if they could never be overcome.

But God just laughs and shows us that the very idea that problems could defeat His children is laughable. If we would only focus more on our Father and His greatness, we could laugh through every trial and test of life, laughing and speaking to the problems, to the mountains in our lives to get out of the way.

When God fills you with His joy, there is nothing in this world that can disturb that joy. When God fills you with rejoicing, no circumstance and no person alive can prevent you from rejoicing. When God makes you laugh, nothing can steal your victory.

The God of laughter is in us, and He is *"greater"*:

> *Ye are of God, little children, and have overcome them: because greater is He that is in you, than he that is in the world.*   1 John 4:4

Because God is in us and He is *"greater,"* we have every reason to laugh, to rejoice.

God promises to *"compass"* us *"with a shield"*:

> *For Thou, LORD, wilt bless the righteous; with favour wilt Thou compass him as with a shield.*
> Psalm 5:12

That word *compass* means "to circle about, enclose." God's shield of protection is all around us. Why should we be afraid? Why should we fail to rejoice?

God has promised to provide *"a lamp unto [our] feet, and a light unto [our] path"*:

Thy word is a lamp unto my feet, and a light unto my path.   Psalm 119:105

What do we have to fear? God is with us. He is guiding our paths. He is giving us light. He will not allow us to stumble. No wonder He laughs! We should too.

The Living Bible version of Psalm 2:4 is interesting:

> *But God in heaven merely laughs! He is amused by all their puny plans.*

God is *"amused,"* and we should be too. How dare wicked men think that they can defeat the power of the Living God! How dare wicked men think that they can defeat the children of the Living God! We have a right to be amused at their *"puny plans."* We are not destined for defeat; we are destined for greatness. We are not destined to lose; we are destined to win. God has chosen us, not to be *"the tail,"* but to be *"the head"*:

> *And the LORD shall make thee the head, and not the tail; and thou shalt be above only, and thou shalt not be beneath; if that thou hearken unto the commandments of the LORD thy God, which I command thee this day, to observe and to do them.*   Deuteronomy 28:13

No wonder the Lord laughs at the wicked who plot to destroy us! He knows our destiny. We should laugh too.

When we laugh with God, we are not laughing at the misfortune of men. We are laughing because of the promise of God. We are laughing because the future is secure in Him. We are laughing because He is our Father and we are His children and because we know how much He loves us.

Instead of worrying about what evil men are doing, spend that time praising and worshipping God. Spend that time rejoicing in Him. Spend that time laughing with the joy of the Lord.

Whatever men plot against us will come to *"naught,"* to nothing. Rejoice! Laugh in faith!

If God is laughing about all this, why are we crying? If God is laughing about all this, what are we worried about? If God is laughing about all this, why should we be so concerned? God's promises never fail. His Word cannot *"return void."* Laugh in the face of every difficulty. I encourage you to check your joy thermometer today and yield to the ministry of the Holy Spirit, that He may fill your sails with the wind of God, carrying you fully into God's presence in joy and laughter.

Sometimes trouble seems to flood in upon us and overwhelm us. Still God is not disturbed. He laughs. He knows the end of all things. He knows who wins.

One of the areas in which we often feel over-whelmed is with our finances and the many demands made upon us from day to day. We need to laugh off these heavy burdens and not allow them to weigh us down.

Another of those areas in which we are easily over-whelmed is with our children, the things they face in a changing world and the challenge to make the right decisions for them from moment to moment. God knows how hard it is to be a parent in the twenty-first century. He wants us to laugh off these heavy burdens and trust Him to give our children victory.

Marriage, the changing roles of spouses and the challenge of keeping a sacred union intact and fresh is another area that can easily overwhelm us these days. Laugh it off, enter into God's presence with joy, and He will give you victory.

Other relationships — with co-workers, with neighbors, with siblings or with aging parents, for example — often bring overwhelming floods of negative emotion flowing over us. These are not easy issues, and they require a LOT of wisdom, but God's wisdom says that we should laugh these burdens off and be free to obey Him.

Sometimes we feel so overwhelmed by the circum-stances of our lives that we want to just lay down and give up. The enemy of our souls loves that. It's exactly what he wants. God, however, wants us to laugh and skip and sing like carefree children right into His presence. He wants us to realize that He is greater than any burden, any struggle, any failure and that we have complete victory in Him.

It is time to stop allowing Satan to rob us of our joy. Don't let a thief come into your house and carry your joy away through unbelief. Refuse to let him take your joy and laughter from you. If you give the enemy space, he will take advantage of it. If you give him room, he will occupy it. If you give him an opportunity, he will not waste it. He's good at what he does, so don't give him a place in your life. Laugh him away from your door. He can't stand the joy and laughter of the Lord.

Satan would like to keep you from growing up, from realizing your true potential in God. He would like to keep you on the bottle the rest of your life. He doesn't want you to take your rightful place in the Kingdom of God, and He knows that if he can keep you from getting a revelation of the power of God and what it can do through you, he can keep you right where he wants you.

When you come into the revelation of who you are in God, when it becomes *rhema* in your heart, it is life-changing. There's no holding you back. When you realize your place in the Kingdom, you become unstoppable. Satan will do anything to prevent that from happening. He doesn't want you to know the truth, that ignorance is not bliss and that your Father has you by the hand.

It is time for you to listen to Father and hear His plan for your life. Then, when you have heard it, you can start laughing. As children of the King, we have every right to be joyful. We have every right to sing and dance and rejoice. We have every right to laugh. There is no reason for us to be defeated. We need to take a good long look at our Jewish roots and our Jewish brethren. They know how to celebrate and enter into God's presence in joy, laughter, singing, praising, worshiping and dancing before the Lord in freedom and liberty. As God has said in His Word:

> *Praise ye the LORD. Sing unto the LORD a new song, and His praise in the congregation of saints. Let Israel rejoice in Him that made him: let the children of Zion be joyful in their King. Let them praise His name in the dance: let them sing praises unto Him with the timbrel and harp. For the LORD taketh pleasure in His people: He will beautify the meek with salvation. Let the saints be joyful in glory: let them sing aloud upon their beds. Let the high praises of God be in their mouth, and a twoedged sword in their hand.* Psalm 149:1-6

We are co-heirs with Christ Jesus. We are in blood covenant with God. What is His is ours, and what is ours is His. Get the revelation. Let a *rhema* word come into your spirit, and let it become life to you. Let the wind of God's Spirit stir up the embers in your soul. Allow Him to breathe new life into your dreams that seem to be going nowhere at the moment. Allow Him to chart the course of your destiny:

> *Arise, shine; for thy light is come, and the glory of the* Lord *is risen upon thee.*   Isaiah 60:1

Refuse to allow the enemy to rob you of your vision. Don't permit him to take from you the dreams God has given you for your life. Fulfill your destiny. Because God laughs, you can too.

When God sees us, He doesn't see weak individuals prone to failure; He sees overcomers. His Word declares it:

> *Nay, in all these things we are MORE THAN CONQUERORS through Him that loved us.*
> Romans 8:37

"More than conquerors!" Think about it.

What is a conqueror? It is "a person who overcomes, a person who defeats, subdues, reduces, overcomes, overthrows by force or strategy." And God said that we are MORE than that. Glory to God!

If God sees us as overcomers, as *"more than conquerors,"* then it is time that we started acting like it. Since He has declared that we, in fact, ARE *"more than conquerors,"* it's time that we started to act the part. Get a vision of your destiny and begin to laugh in the face of the enemy. God keeps things simple for His children. We're the ones who complicate everything. Please don't let anyone discourage you from the joy and laughter of the Lord.

Joy is very important to us. It is one of our most powerful weapons. We must not allow anyone to steal it from us. We must focus on the Source of our joy and stop focusing on the circumstances of life. God laughs at His enemies, and He has called us to laugh too.

Far too many of God's children are hiding in some corner having a pity party. Far too many are running away from life's battles with their tail between their legs. Far too many are caught up in their woe-is-me attitude. It is time to arise and shake off the negative influences around us, shake off the grave clothes and put on the garments of praise, joy and laughter. Let us be the men and women God has called us to be. Let us be what God's infallible and uncontrovertible Word says we already are.

We all have enemies. That's just a part of life. David, as sweet and innocent as he was, had his enemies. The most serious of those enemies was

King Saul himself. Despite the fact that David had done the king so much good, Saul turned on him and persecuted him mercilessly. Psalm 59 was written during a time when soldiers had been sent by the king to find David and kill him. Under the constant pressure of this persecution from the most powerful man in the land, David prayed:

> *O my God, save me from my enemies.*
> *Protect me from these who have come to destroy me.*
> *Preserve me from these criminals, these murders.*
> *They lurk in ambush for my life.*
> *Strong men are out there waiting.*
> *And not, O Lord, because I've done them wrong.*
> *Yet they prepare to kill me.*
>
> Psalm 59:1-4, TLB

David had done nothing wrong that would merit such treatment. He did not deserve to be kicked and knocked down. Why was it happening? That's just the way Satan is. He doesn't need an excuse. He hated David because he was a child of God. That was excuse enough. That's the way he is. That's the way he acts, and, child of God, Satan hates you too. Don't be deceived.

David was sure that God would want to come to his rescue as he stirred himself in prayer. He continued his prayer:

> *Lord, Awaken! See what is happening! Help me!*
> *(And O Jehovah, God of heaven's armies,*
> *God of Israel, arise and punish the heathen nations surrounding us.)*
> *Do not spare these evil, treacherous men.*
> *At evening they come to spy, slinking around like dogs that prowl the city.*
> *I hear them shouting insults and cursing God, for "No one will hear us," they think.*
>
> Psalm 59:4-7, TLB

What did David suppose that God would do in that moment? He prayed earnestly:

> *Lord, laugh at them!*
> *(And scoff at these surrounding nations too.)*
>
> Psalm 59:8, TLB

David was sure that God would want to laugh at the *"puny plans"* of his enemies, and he was laughing himself.

David had been anointed by the prophet Samuel to be the next king of Israel. How could anyone kill him before his time? How could anyone keep him from his time? How could anyone keep him from his destiny? Saul's threats were funny. They could not possibly prosper — even if he was the king, even if he did have armies to carry out his commands.

David knew whom he was serving, and those who serve the God above all other gods cannot fail. Our God is a mighty Deliverer. He is *"the lifter up of my head"*:

> *But thou, O LORD, art a shield for me; my glory, and the lifter up of mine head.*
> *I cried unto the LORD with my voice, and He heard me out of His holy hill. Selah.*
>
> Psalm 3:3-4

It was David who first sang these words. He received this revelation. He knew who God was. He knew that his God would never bow the knee to Baal or any other god and that he could not be defeated by any man.

David understood his covenant rights. He was in partnership with the Almighty, and no one — however powerful — could do him harm. He knew that God would deliver him, so he laughed in the face of Saul's threats, and he knew that God would want to join him in that laughter, creating Heaven's atmosphere right where he was.

Jesus paid for our deliverance with His own blood on the cross. Why should we not be free? Jesus conquered death, Hell and the grave. Why should we be dragged down to eternal punishment by the devil? Through the blood of Jesus, deliverance is ours. Let us rejoice and be glad. Let us laugh at the enemy of our souls. God is on our side. We cannot be defeated.

Not only does God laugh, but all of Heaven laughs with Him. The Scriptures declare, for instance, that when a soul is saved, all hosts of Heaven rejoice:

> *I say unto you, that likewise joy shall be in heaven over one sinner that repenteth.*
>
> Luke 15:7

Heaven is a joyful place, and the inhabitants of Heaven are constantly rejoicing. How much more should we rejoice? If all of Heaven laughs, then surely we have a right to laugh too, and we should laugh, full of joy, our cups overflowing, affecting those around us for good.

TWO

WHY BELIEVERS LAUGH

Then Abraham fell upon his face, and LAUGHED, and said in his heart, Shall a child be born unto him that is an hundred years old? and shall Sarah, that is ninety years old, bear?

Genesis 17:17

As we have seen, we, as believers, have every right to laugh. God is our Father; we are heirs to His riches; He guards and protects us from every enemy. Rather than ask why we laugh, we should ask 'Why not laugh?' We have every right to laugh.

Not every laugh of the believer, however, is wholesome. The Bible gives us examples of those who laughed in unbelief. Even Abraham, the father of our faith, was among them. What God promised him was so awesome, so unbelievable, that his faith wavered for a moment. He was incredulous, which means "skeptical, disbelieving, expressive of disbelief."

Can you blame Abraham? After all, what God said was rather unbelievable, rather incredible. This word incredible means "too unlikely to be believed, unbelievable, extraordinary, astonishing." What God said to Abraham was certainly incredible. It was difficult to grasp with the natural mind. It's not every day, after all, that people as old as Abraham and Sarah are able to bear a child.

When God said it, Abraham did the right thing in one sense. He threw himself down in worship before the Lord, but inside he was laughing in disbelief. "Me, a father? At a hundred years old? Sarah, a mother? At ninety?" I can hear him saying it.

Sarah was no different. The whole thing was incredible to her way of thinking, just as it had been to Abraham, and she too laughed:

> So Sarah laughed silently. "A woman my age have a baby?" she scoffed to herself. "And with a husband as old as mine?"
>
> Genesis 18:12, TLB

The patriarchs were very human. They were real people, flesh and blood, no different from you and me.

We can understand what Sarah was feeling. She and Abraham were getting up in years, and not everything about their bodies was in working order. Sarah had experienced menopause long before this and was now way past the normal age of child-bearing.

That's how God does His wonders. He waits until we cannot possibly receive the credit for something ourselves, and then He does it. No one could have denied the miracle of Isaac's birth. It was impossible to refute, and God did it this way because He desires to have all the glory. He shares it with no man.

God wasn't happy with Sarah's laugh of incredulity:

> *Then God said to Abraham, "Why did Sarah laugh? Why did she say 'Can an old woman like me have a baby?' Is anything too hard for God? Next year, just as I told you, I will certainly see to it that Sarah has a son."*
> Genesis 18:13-14, TLB

Sarah, of course, denied the fact that she had laughed at all. She was afraid, so she lied:

> *But Sarah denied it. "I didn't laugh," she lied, for she was afraid.* Genesis 18:15, TLB

Fear causes us to do funny things. It is the opposite of faith. We must be truthful before God, recognizing our lack of faith and allowing Him to place within us the true joy that will cause us to laugh for Him.

In the end, Sarah did laugh with joy and not with unbelief:

> *And Sarah declared, "God has brought me laughter! All who hear about this shall rejoice with me. For who would have dreamed that I would ever have a baby? Yet I have given Abraham a child in his old age!"*
>
> Genesis 21:6-7, TLB

Why could Sarah laugh? God put joy and laughter in her. God had performed His word, and the miracle of it brought great delight to her heart. Beloved, this is God's kind of laughter. This is God's kind of joy. This is a laughter and a joy of which the world can have no understanding.

Sarah was so full of joy that she laughed because God had done exactly as He had promised. He had said that He would give Abraham a baby boy in his old age, and in order to do that the elderly Sarah had to conceive. That seemed incredible, impossible, but it happened nevertheless. Our God is faithful to His word, and He brought it to pass.

When the miraculous child of Abraham and Sarah was born, the name given to him was *Isaac* which means "laughter." What a strange name for a child! Laughter!

Abraham and Sarah had laughter because God is the God of laughter. They had laughter because God fulfills His promises. They had laughter because nothing is too hard for God.

The year Isaac was born, Abraham became a centenarian. He was one hundred years old. No wonder the two of them laughed! No wonder Sarah marveled: *"Who would have dreamt ... ?"* God has some great surprises in store for you and me as well. He has ordained that believers laugh for joy, not with unbelief, and He provides the miracle-working power that causes us to rejoice and be overcomers, for laughter is the key to overcoming.

God's power in us will be a testimony to all the nations:

> *How we laughed and sang for joy.*
> *And the other nations said, "What amazing things the Lord has done for them."*
> Psalm 126:2, TLB

When we laugh with joy, the people around us sit up and take notice. Laughing is an outward expression of something wonderful that is taking place on the inside. It represents a spirit brought to life. It is a wholesome and challenging testimony to all those who hear it. It is a sign and a wonder to the world.

This psalm begins with the words:

> *When Jehovah brought back His exiles to Jerusalem, it was like a dream!*
> Psalm 126:1, TLB

Being loosed from captivity was no small thing, and being returned to the Holy City was cause for rejoicing. No wonder they sang for joy! No wonder they laughed! No wonder those around them were amazed! This is the joy of the Lord.

The psalmist continued:

> *Yes, glorious things! What wonder! What joy!*
> *May we be refreshed as by streams in the desert.*
> Verse 3, TLB

As we shall see later in the book, there is a time for weeping. The psalmist shows us:

> *Those who sow tears shall reap joy. Yes, they go out weeping, carrying seed for sowing, and return singing, carrying their sheaves.*
> Verses 5-6, TLB

The weeping was clearly meant to be temporary, and the will of God for His people is rejoicing. Those who go forth *"weeping"* will return *"singing."*

Jesus taught His disciples:

> *What happiness there is for you who are now hungry, for you are going to be satisfied! What happiness there is for you who weep, for the time will come when you shall laugh with joy! What happiness it is when others hate you and exclude you and insult you and smear your name because you are mine! When that happens, rejoice! Yes, leap for joy! For you will have a great reward awaiting you in heaven. And you will be in good company — the ancient prophets were treated that way too!*
>
> Luke 6:21-23, TLB

In the King James Version this portion of the Sermon on the Mount reads like this:

> *And He lifted up His eyes on His disciples, and said, Blessed be ye poor: for yours is the kingdom of God. Blessed are ye that hunger now: for ye shall be filled. Blessed are ye that weep now: for ye shall laugh. Blessed are ye, when men shall hate you, and when they shall separate you from their company, and shall reproach*

you, and cast out your name as evil, for the Son of man's sake. Rejoice ye in that day, and leap for joy: for, behold, your reward is great in heaven: for in the like manner did their fathers unto the prophets. Luke 6:20-23

If we remain humble and continually hunger for God we are promised a great future. Those who have wept can start laughing. Even when men severely persecute us we can rejoice.

What did Jesus say to do in that day? *Rejoice ... and leap for joy.* This is a time for joy and for the demonstration of joy to the world around us.

No one has fallen so far that Jesus cannot lift them up again. If we will only yield to Him, He will minister to us by His sweet Spirit, calm all the hurts and disappointments of the past and fill us with His laughter, with *"joy unspeakable and full of glory."*

What should prevent us from being joyful, from laughing? He has said, *"Great is your reward."* What could be more wonderful? We have every reason to rejoice.

We know the end of the story. We win; we have the last laugh:

And now the righteous shall see them destroyed; the innocent shall laugh the wicked to scorn.

"See," they will say, "the last of our enemies have been destroyed in the fire."

Job 22:19-20, TLB

The followers of God will see it happen. They will watch in awe. Then they will laugh and say, "See what happens to those who despise God and trust in their wealth, and become ever more bold in their wickedness."

Psalm 52:6-7, TLB

What will we see? We will see God exercising judgment upon the wicked. He said to them:

But God will strike you down and pull you from your home, and drag you away from the land of the living. Verse 5, TLB

Unlike the believer (who has nothing to fear and every reason to rejoice), those who love wickedness, who love lying, who love slander and who delight in harming others have much to fear and nothing at all to laugh about. This brings us to our next subject: Why Unbelievers Laugh.

THREE

WHY UNBELIEVERS LAUGH

Who is it you scoffed against and mocked? Whom did you revile? At whom did you direct your violence and pride? It was against the Holy One of Israel. You have sent your messengers to mock the Lord.

Isaiah 37:23-24, TLB

The unbeliever dares to laugh at God, even to mock Christ:

Everyone who sees me mocks and sneers and shrugs. "Is this the one who rolled his burden on the Lord?" they laugh. "Is this the one who claims the Lord delights in him? We'll believe it when we see God rescue him!"

Psalm 22:7-8, TLB

This was not just a one-time occurrence. Men laughed at Christ often:

> *When Jesus arrived at the rabbi's home and saw the noisy crowds and heard the funeral music, he said, "Get them out, for the little girl isn't dead; she's only sleeping!" Then how they all scoffed and sneered at Him.*
>
> Matthew 9:23-24, TLB

These men refused to believe that Jesus was capable of giving life to the dead. He put them out because they were unworthy to witness the miracle He was about to do. They were blinded by the god of this world.

In the King James Version, this latter part of the verse reads:

> *He said unto them, Give place: for the maid is not dead, but sleepeth. And they laughed Him to scorn.* Matthew 9:24

What arrogance for men to laugh at God! No wonder Hell awaits them if they don't repent and receive the Lord Jesus Christ as Lord and Savior in their lives.

In exactly the same way unbelievers laugh at God, they also laugh at God's children. They can't understand us, so they have to try to make us appear foolish. Their laughter is also an attempt to intimidate us.

When Nehemiah was called of God to organize and oversee the rebuilding of the walls and gates of Jerusalem, the unbelievers in the area were quite amused:

> *But when Sanballat and Tobiah and Geshem the Arab heard of our plan, they scoffed and said, "What are you doing, rebelling against the king like this?"*
> *But I replied, "The God of heaven will help us, and we, His servants, will rebuild this wall; but you may have no part in this affair."*
>   Nehemiah 2:19-20, TLB

When Nehemiah got to Jerusalem, he found that circumstances were not favorable to his project. Everything and everyone seemed to be against him. Nehemiah, however, had a vision and a desire to be faithful to that vision, and he could not be easily swayed to give up what was on his heart to do. He was fully persuaded in his heart.

The unbelievers could not understand Nehemiah's vision, and they wanted no part of it. They did feel compelled to stop long enough to scoff at him. Unbelievers have always been good at this.

They are not willing to lend a hand, but they will stay around long enough to criticize and laugh at you.

The Bible records the burden of Nehemiah in these words:

> *Then said I unto them, Ye see the distress that we are in, how Jerusalem lieth waste, and the gates thereof are burned with fire: come, and let us build up the wall of Jerusalem, that we be no more a reproach. Then I told them of the hand of my God which was good upon me; as also the king's words that he had spoken unto me. And they said, Let us rise up and build. So they strengthened their hands for this good work.*
>
> Nehemiah 2:17-18

Nehemiah had a burden, and that burden was imparted to his fellow believers. The unbelievers considered it to be nonsense. This happens to us all too often with our family members, our friends or our co-workers. They just look at us like we're crazy, but we know who wins in the end. Unbelievers may mock now, but a day of reckoning is coming if they fail to repent.

No wonder unbelievers can't understand us! We live in another world. We are as different from them as night and day — literally — and people have always criticized what they cannot understand. Because unbelievers are walking dead men, they can't understand the things of life.

The King James Version of the Bible records the unbeliever's reaction to Nehemiah in these words:

> *But when Sanballat the Horonite, and Tobiah the servant, the Ammonite, and Geshem the Arabian, heard it, they laughed us to scorn, and despised us, and said, What is this thing that ye do? will ye rebel against the king?*
> *Then answered I them, and said unto them, The God of heaven, He will prosper us; therefore we His servants will arise and build: but ye have no portion, nor right, nor memorial, in Jerusalem.*   Nehemiah 2:19-20

There could be no better picture of the unbeliever. That's exactly what they are like. They laugh at Christ and at His followers.

Job, a righteous man, became *"a laughingstock"* to his neighbors. He said:

> *And who doesn't know these things you've been saying? I, the man who begged God for help, and God answered him, have became a laughingstock to my neighbors. Yes, I, a righteous man, am now the man they scoff at. Meanwhile, the*

rich mock those in trouble and are quick to despise all those in need. For robbers prosper. Go ahead and provoke God — it makes no difference! He will supply your every need anyway!

Job 12:3-6, TLB

The King James Version says it this way:

I am as one mocked of his neighbour, who calleth upon God, and He answereth him: the just upright man is laughed to scorn.   Job 12:4

Some of us are highly esteemed in certain localities or nations within the family of God. Still we are despised by unbelievers. They even consider us to be dangerous.

Don't look to the world for help. Men will just laugh at you.

Again, it needs to be said that unregenerate men only laugh at us because the devil, their father, laughs at us. He is the true mocker, the true scorner of everyone and everything good and holy. Get filled with God's joy, and nothing that men or devils can do will rob you of your laughter.

Don't expect to be praised by men. Many scriptural passages teach us to expect the opposite and to be ready for it:

WHY UNBELIEVERS LAUGH

Thou makest us a strife unto our neighbours:
and our enemies laugh among themselves.
Psalm 80:6

The Living Bible gives the same verse in these words:

And have made us the scorn of the neighboring
nations. They laugh among themselves.
Psalm 80:6, TLB

Unbelievers will take every opportunity to laugh at Christ, at His followers and at His teachings, His ordinances. It happened to King Hezekiah. He and his advisors agreed to call everyone to a solemn assembly in Jerusalem:

King Hezekiah now sent letters throughout all
of Israel, Judah, Ephraim and Manasseh, invit-
ing everyone to come to the Temple at Jerusalem
for the annual Passover celebration. The king,
his aids, and all the assembly of Jerusalem had
voted to celebrate the Passover in May this time
rather than at the normal time in April, because
not enough Priests were sanctified at the ear-
lier date, and there wasn't enough time to get
notices out. The king and his advisors were in
complete agreement in this matter. So they sent

a Passover proclamation throughout Israel, from Dan to Beer-sheba inviting, everyone. They had not kept it in great numbers as prescribed. 2 Chronicles 30:1-5, TLB

The letter they sent out said this:

"Come back to the Lord God of Abraham, Isaac and Israel ... so that He will return to us who have escaped from the power of the kings of Assyria. Do not be like your fathers and brothers who sinned against the Lord God of their fathers and were destroyed. Do not be stubborn, as they were, but yield yourselves to the Lord and come to His Temple which He has sanctified forever, and worship the Lord your God so that His fierce anger will turn away from you. For if you turn to the Lord again, your brothers and your children will be treated mercifully by their captors, and they will be able to return to this land. For the Lord your God is full of kindness and mercy and will not continue to turn away His face from you if you return to Him." 2 Chronicles 30:6-9, TLB

This message was taken from city to city *"as far as Zebulon"* (Verse 10, TLB), but, for the most part, it was met with scorn. The King James Version says it like this:

> *So the posts passed from city to city through the country of Ephraim and Manasseh even unto Zebulun; but they laughed them to scorn, and mocked them.* 2 Chronicles 30:10

Hezekiah could have gotten discouraged with this turn of events and given up, but he didn't, and we must not get discouraged either. Overlook unbelievers. They don't understand what they are doing. You do the right thing — whether people understand you or not. Keep praising God and keep peace and joy in your heart — whether others do or not. You will win in the end.

Eventually there was a favorable response to the letter Hezekiah sent out:

> *However, some of the tribes of Asher, Manasseh, and Zebulun turned to God and came to Jerusalem. But in Judah the entire nation felt a strong, God-given desire to obey the Lord's direction as commanded by the king and his officers. And so it was that a very large crowd assembled at Jerusalem in the month of May for the Passover celebration.*
> 2 Chronicles 30:11-13, TLB

TICKLE ME SILLY, GOD

God will always have a remnant of people who will obey Him. Just make sure you are not among the mockers and scorners, for to laugh at God's ordinances is a pretty stupid thing to do.

Eventually the unbeliever's laugh of scorn will vanish from his lips, and it will be God's turn to laugh:

> *I also will laugh at your calamity; I will mock when your fear cometh.*   Proverbs 1:26

These are pretty strong words. The Living Bible says it this way:

> *Some day you'll be in trouble, and I'll laugh!*
> *Mock Me, will you? — I'll mock you.*
>   Proverbs 1:26, TLB

May God help us. It doesn't pay to mock Him.

Solomon, the wise King of Israel and the son of David, wrote most of what makes up the book of Proverbs. He wanted to teach his people how to live, how to act properly in every circumstance. He wanted them to be just and fair in everything they did. He wanted to warn young men about some of the temptations they would face in life. He wanted to help make even those he called *"the simple minded"* wise. He wanted those who were already wise to become even wiser, so that they could become leaders among their people. He wanted his ministry to the people to multiply. In Proverbs, he discussed in depth the subject of wisdom and how one may obtain it. His conclusion was this:

> *How does a man become wise? The first step is to trust and reverence the Lord!*
> Proverbs 1:7, TLB

Other proverbs agree:

> *The fear of the LORD is the beginning of wisdom: and the knowledge of the holy is understanding.* Proverbs 9:10

> *For the reverence and fear of God are basic to all wisdom. Knowing God results in every other kind of understanding.* Proverbs 9:10, TLB

So if the reverence of the Lord is so important, what will be the end of those who mock and scorn Him?

Solomon continued in that first proverb:

> *Only fools refuse to be taught. Listen to your father and mother. What you learn from them*

*will stand you in good stead; it will gain you
many honors.*   Proverbs 1:7-9, TLB

Some of what Solomon taught in Proverbs sounds
like it could have been clipped from our daily news-
papers or excerpted from an evening television
newscast in most any one of our cities:

*If young toughs tell you, "Come and join us"
— turn your back on them! "We'll hide and
rob and kill," they say. "Good or bad, we'll treat
them all alike. And the loot we'll get! All kinds
of stuff! Come on, throw in your lot with us;
we'll split with you in equal shares."
Don't do it, son! Stay far from men like that,
for crime is their way of life, and murder is their
specialty. When a bird sees a trap being set, it
stays away, but not these men; they trap themselves! They lay a booby-trap for their own lives.
Such is the fate of all who live by violence and
murder. They will die a violent death.*
                              Proverbs 1:10-19, TLB

Such are the fools who laugh at God. They don't
even know that they are setting traps for themselves.
We must rescue people like these and bring them
out of darkness and into the light of the Kingdom
of God. He declares in His Word that the heathen

are our inheritance; do let us lay hold of them in faith.

Solomon clarified further the dismal status of such people:

> *Wisdom shouts in the streets for a hearing. She calls out to the crowds along Main Street, and to the judges in their courts, and to everyone in all the land: "You simpletons!" she cries. "How long will you go on being fools? How long will you scoff at wisdom and fight the facts? Come here and listen to me! I'll pour out the spirit of wisdom upon you, and make you wise. I have called you so often but still you won't come. I have pleaded, but all in vain. For you have spurned my counsel and reproof."*
>
> Proverbs 1:20-25, TLB

What a sad state of affairs. These people are *"simpletons."* They are *"fools."* They have spurned *"the counsel and reproof"* of the Lord. It was then, after having said all this, that the Lord spoke those very harsh words: *Some day you'll be in trouble, and I'll laugh! Mock me, will you? — I'll mock you.*

It is time to call men everywhere to repentance, for those who have mocked God and spurned His counsel will not prosper. God has declared that He will not tolerate the mocking of His creation:

TiCKLE ME SiLLY, GOD

Be not deceived; God is not mocked: for what-soever a man soweth, that shall he also reap.
Galatians 6:7

God must be respected. The harsh words contin-ued:

When a storm of terror surrounds you, and when you are engulfed by anguish and distress, then I will not answer your cry for help. It will be too late though you search for Me ever so anxiously. Proverbs 1:27-28, TLB

TOO LATE! What terrible words! Men who mock God will one day wake to find that it is TOO LATE for repentance, TOO LATE to change, TOO LATE to answer God's call.

God isn't to blame. He has been more than gra-cious to men everywhere. He said:

For you closed your eyes to the facts and did not choose to reverence and trust the Lord, and you turned your back on Me, spurning my ad-vice. That is why you must eat the bitter fruit of having your own way, and experience the full terrors of the pathway you have chosen. For you have turned away from Me — to death; your own complacency will kill you. Fools! But all who listen to Me shall live in peace and safety, unafraid.   Proverbs 1:29-33, TLB

FOOLS! What damning words!

What is the complacency of which this proverb speaks. It is "self-satisfaction accompanied by unawareness of actual dangers or deficiencies." That sounds like most unbelievers I know. They cannot accept that God has placed an immutable law in the land: what you reap, you sow. Those who reject God will be rejected by God. Those who laugh at Him will be laughed at in their day of calamity. Not to believe it is to be a *simpleton.*

It may seem to us at times like sinners are prospering. We may see them feasting, laughing, enjoying their worldly pleasures and be tempted to join them. Jesus said that all their merriment would come to a tragic end:

> *But woe unto you that are rich! for ye have received your consolation. Woe unto you that are full! for ye shall hunger. Woe unto you that laugh now! for ye shall mourn and weep. Woe unto you, when all men shall speak well of you! for so did their fathers to the false prophets.*
>   Luke 6:24-26

The Beatitudes have become one of the most well known and beloved passages of sacred Scripture.

They contain Jesus' formula for blessing. They also contain, however, His formula for cursing. The "blesseds" are for the believers, and the "woes" are for the unbelievers.

The Living Bible presents this same passage in this way:

> *But, oh, the sorrows that await the rich. For they have their only happiness down here. They are fat and prosperous now, but a time of awful hunger is before them. Their careless laughter now means sorrow then. And what sadness is ahead for those praised by the crowds — for false prophets have always been praised.*
>
> Luke 6:24-26, TLB

Jesus exhorted believers to be good to *"fools,"* to those who reject Christ. He said to us:

> *Listen, all of you, love your enemies. Do good to those who hate you. Pray for the happiness of those who curse you; implore God's blessings on those who hurt you.*
>
> Luke 6:27-28, TLB

It takes a big man or woman to do it, but the rewards are great.

FOUR

WHAT IS FALSE LAUGHTER?

Even in laughter the heart is sorrowful; and the end of that mirth is heaviness.

Proverbs 14:13

Laughing is fun. We all like to laugh and, because of that, the entertainment industry is one of the largest industries in our country and the world. Laughter, however, has its limitations. It cannot satisfy. Only Jesus can do that.

Solomon learned this lesson during his exhaustive search for happiness:

I said to myself, "Come now, be merry; enjoy yourself to the full." But I found that this, too,

was futile. For it is silly to be laughing all the time; what good does it do?
Ecclesiastes 2:1, TLB

True and lasting joy and laughter only come from God and are the fruit of His Spirit. We cannot get true joy packaged any other way. We cannot achieve it through the world's methods. True and lasting joy is not to be found in the world.

The laughter of the world is vain. It doesn't last. It doesn't satisfy us for long. Solomon also wrote:

A party gives laughter, and wine gives happiness, and money gives everything!
Ecclesiastes 10:19, TLB

Let's think about that for a moment. In the world, men drink to get happy and laugh. God has taught us Christians, however, that drink and drunkenness lead to *debauchery*, "an extreme indulgence in sensuality." An extreme form of this phenomena results in orgies. God wants us to be filled with another type of Spirit, His Holy Spirit. He said:

And be not drunk with wine, wherein is excess; but be filled with the Spirit;
Ephesians 5:18

WHAT IS FALSE LAUGHTER?

The laughter that comes from drunkenness is temporary, very short-lived. And, because it does not result in life, the end of such activities is often tragic.

Don't waste your time seeking joy among those who reject God. They are *"rebels"* and *"fools"*:

> *To do right honors God; to sin is to despise Him.*
> *A rebel's foolish talk should prick his own pride!*
> *But the wise man's speech is respected.*
>   Proverbs 14:2-3, TLB

We have no place in the haunts of unbelievers. They live in another world, a world we have examined and found wanting. While the ways of the world seem right to men, we know that the end of those ways is *"death"*:

> *There is a way which seemeth right unto a man,*
> *but the end thereof are the ways of death.*
>   Proverbs 14:12

Carnal laughter may temporarily mask a heavy heart, but when the laughter ends, the grief remains. This type of laughter is vain.

When I was living in sin as a backslider, I put on a good show, just like everyone else. I laughed on the outside, but I was crying on the inside. What a miserable person I was! I knew that I wasn't where

I should be, yet I kept trying to find happiness apart from God. The harder I tried, the more I cried on the inside.

Did I have fun? Yes, I did. Sin is fun. The problem is that the fun we experience with sin doesn't last. It quickly passes. Then the results of sin begin to take their toll on our lives. Sin leaves us with a bad taste in our mouths, with a headache or hangover and with a guilty conscience. When it's over, it's all over. "The wages of sin is death."

There is a saying: Sin will always take you farther than you wanted to go. It will always keep you longer than you wanted to stay. It will always cost you more than you were willing to pay. Those who are wise will depart from sin and return to the arms of the Almighty, for only He has true and lasting joy to offer.

Backsliders are the most miserable people of all. They know what it is to have the blessing of God, and they get bored with sin very quickly. They are constantly searching for something to fill the void. Their laughter is nothing more than a masquerade. Underneath they are hurting people.

The world seems to be full of laughter, but this kind of laughter will lead you straight to the gates of Hell. *"Come out from among them,"* the Lord has said (2 Corinthians 6:17). Make your decision today to reject the false and to seek God for genuine joy and laughter.

FiVE

WHEN I BEGAN TO LAUGH IN THE SPIRIT

O the depth of the riches both of the wisdom and knowledge of God! how unsearchable are His judgments, and His ways past finding out!
Romans 11:33

On April 1, 1986, God baptized me in the Holy Spirit with the evidence of speaking in other tongues and, at the same time, called me into the ministry. It happened in my laundry room as I was speaking with a prayer partner from The 700 Club, and what an awesome experience it was! A heavy weight, much like chains, was lifted from me that day, I was flooded with God's joy, and I began to laugh. I laughed and I laughed and I laughed some more. I was silly with laughter. At that moment, the phone rang and it was my husband. He wanted to know what was wrong with me. His first thought was that I had overdosed on my medication.

Knowing how he hated anything that had to do with God, I started to lie to him, just so he would not pursue the matter further, but I found that I could no longer lie. I prayed, "Lord, what am I to say to him?"

The Lord said, "Ask him if he knows what the baptism of the Holy Spirit is."

I asked him, and he said "no."

"Tell him then," the Lord continued, "that he would not understand what has happened."

When I told him this, he said, "Oh," and changed the subject. From that time on, you could have tortured me, and I would not have lied. It was a manifestation of the baptism of the Spirit of Truth I had received.

The laughter I was experiencing went on for many days. Every time the Spirit of the Lord would move upon me, I would be flooded with joy and laughter. It was not that I was idle or doing nothing else. I was moving ahead with my life, standing in the trenches and facing the daily battles that are common to those who choose the Christian life. Still, sometime in the course of each day, the Holy Spirit would move upon me, I would fall forward on my face before the Lord, and the Spirit would again flood me with joy and laughter. I would be silly with laughter.

The experience continues to this day, and now I see that God is doing this miracle for many other believers in different parts of our country and the world. Nothing could be more wonderful than the joy of the Lord. It is, as the prophet showed us, our strength:

> *The joy of the LORD is your strength.*
> Nehemiah 8:10

With this, God gave me the revelation that laughter is a powerful weapon of our spiritual warfare against Satan. It represents a release of our faith, and mighty things are accomplished when we give ourselves over to the laughter of the Spirit. I have run with this knowledge, and it has changed my life. The devil had been beating up on me, but now the tables were turned. Hallelujah!

When God called me, He told me that He had given me a ministry that would take me far and wide. I would cross many waters for His glory. The process of my training would be arduous, He told me, but it would be necessary to bring me into the place He wanted me to be spiritually. I understood, again, that His joy and laughter expressed through me would be an awesome weapon of warfare against the enemy.

Job said:

> *Till He fill thy mouth with laughing, and thy lips with rejoicing.*　　　　　Job 8:21

Then, in the late eighties, after a period of much travail in the Spirit, God gave me a vision that deeply impacted my life. I was in a sandy area. As I looked down at my legs and feet, I realized that they were no longer mine, but the Lord's. There were sandals on His feet, and the dust from the road clung to the lower part of His legs. His robe was white, and it was so awesome that I wept, and wept, and wept some more. My heart burned within me, and I knew from that moment on that I could never deny Him and His will for my life — no matter what they cost.

He told me that He was calling and commissioning me, and that He had done this before the foundations of the Earth were laid. He had known me before I was formed in my mother's womb, and, even then, had chosen and ordained me and set His hand upon me.

As I lingered before the Lord in prayer, He showed me areas where He would be sending me as I yielded my life to Him.

I knew that I could do nothing in myself, but since the Lord is all wisdom and knows how to communicate effectively, I could trust Him to give me His message. The Apostle Paul wrote to the Romans:

> *O the depth of the riches both of the wisdom and knowledge of God! how unsearchable are His judgments, and His ways past finding out!*
> Romans 11:33

Our God is a God of love. He desires all the best for us, and He longs to give us the answers we need. He has destined us to greatness even before we knew Him:

> *But God commendeth His love toward us, in that, while we were yet sinners, Christ died for us. Much more then, being now justified by His blood, we shall be saved from wrath through Him.*
> Romans 5:8-9

This word *saved* means "daily delivered from sin's dominion." That is the security we have in the Lord our God.

Our God is present everywhere, always in the NOW, so He is aware of where we are at any given moment, the situations we are encountering right then and what we have need of. We are never alone. The Old Testament assures us:

> *For the eyes of the LORD run to and fro through-*
> *out the whole earth, to shew Himself strong in*
> *the behalf of them whose heart is perfect toward*
> *Him.*   2 Chronicles 16:9

What does God mean by saying that His eyes *"run to and fro throughout the whole earth"*? Since we are created from the earth and are the temple of the Holy Spirit, I feel that He is talking about His constant care over us.

Our God is all knowledge, and He has all the answers we require. Since His understanding is infinite, there is no limitation to what He can show us if we are willing to listen to Him:

> *Great is our Lord, and of great power: His un-*
> *derstanding is infinite.*   Psalm 147:5

Our God is all power, and He has the ability to perform His will. Nothing is too hard for Him:

> *Behold, I am the LORD, the God of all flesh: is*
> *there any thing too hard for Me?*
>   Jeremiah 32:27

Our God is faithful and true. We can trust Him and never be concerned that He will disappoint us. He does what He said He would do:

> *God is not a man, that He should lie; neither the son of man that He should repent: hath He said, and shall He not do it? or hath He spoken, and shall He not make it good?*
>
> Numbers 23:19

Another time, before God sent me to the nations, I had a vision in the night. I was riding in a silver truck, and it stopped. I got out and stood looking out over a dry parched plain. It was so very dry. Then the Lord said, "Look up!" And when I did, I saw fireballs.

I said, "Lord, what is this?"

He said, "Look closer."

I looked up. I could see the stratosphere and I saw these fireballs being thrown through here to the Earth very strategically. They had a purposeful destination. As they passed through the white fluffy clouds of the sky and hit the Earth, it burned wherever they struck.

There were so many of these fireballs I could not count them. I was not afraid, although one of them was thrown right in front of me. The vision ended.

Later, when I was to go the nations, the Lord came

to me while I was in prayer. In His hands was a fireball shaped like a crown. He said, "Take the crown to the nations. You will carry the revival fire with you." Since that time, when I have gone out to the nations for the Lord, He has imparted the fire to others, and they have wept in repentance and wept in joy and laughter, as the Spirit of God burned through and brought revival to their lives, their homes, and the world around them. What an awesome God we serve!

As in my own life, I have discovered that God has a plan for every person's life even before they are born. The psalmist David wrote:

> *My substance was not hid from Thee, when I was made in secret, and curiously wrought in the lowest parts of the earth. Thine eyes did see my substance, yet being unperfect; and in Thy book, all my members were written, which in continuance were fashioned, when as yet there was none of them.* Psalm 139:15-16

How wonderful our Lord is to each of us!

With all of these truths evident, how could I not be joyful? How could I not rejoice? How could I not laugh with glee? It has seemed to me to be a natural part of my Christian experience. While some find it unusual for Christians to laugh, I would find it unusual if they did not.

Even our ministry name reflects this truth. I will never forget the day God dropped the name into my spirit. He told me to call it Joy Ministries. At the time I was very new in the things of the Spirit and had no idea what was going on in other parts of the world. I had no way of knowing that the Holy Spirit was baptizing people in joy all over the world. But it did not surprise me when I heard about it, as it has some. I experienced it, and I continue to experience it to this very day.

Nothing could be more wonderful than the joy of our God and the laughter it produces in our spirits.

PART II

LAUGHTER AND THE FRUITS OF THE SPIRIT

But the fruit of the Spirit is love, joy, peace, longsuffering, gentleness, goodness, faith, meekness, temperance: against such there is no law.
Galatians 5:22-23

SIX

LOVE AND LAUGHTER

But the fruit of the Spirit is LOVE... .
                                        Galatians 5:22

There is a direct link between laughter and the fruit of the Spirit. When we are filled with God's love, His joy, His peace, His longsuffering, His gentleness, His goodness, His faith, His meekness and His temperance, this divine touch overflows and creates within us a well springing up, a well of laughter.

The laughter we experience is a direct result of the Spirit's work in our lives. Although it is not named as one of the nine fruits of the Spirit, laughter is a direct result of the work accomplished by the Spirit of God in us and nothing else. The link between laughter and joy is easy to see, but laughter is linked to all of the other fruits as well.

The fruit of the Spirit is a result of the nature and character of Jesus in the born-again believer. It is not the result of any human effort. As the Living Bible shows, it is only *"when the Holy Spirit controls our lives"* that this fruit can come forth. Only *"He ... produces this kind of fruit."*

Our lives are an extension of Jesus, so the Spirit places within us His very nature and ability so that we can represent Him in the world. He is *"the true vine"* (John 15:1), and we are the branches. Just as a tree is known by its fruit, we are Christians only because the fruit of Christ's nature is evident in our lives, not because we are tagged Christians. The life comes from the vine, but we are blessed because the fruit comes forth on the branches.

Jesus said:

> *Ye shall know them by their fruits.*
>
> Matthew 7:16

The fruits of the Spirit must be evident in the life of the believer on good days and on bad days as well. These fruits must be evident through times of trial and test. Indeed, this is what sets Christians apart from all others. Anyone can be happy when everything is going well, but only true believers can be happy when everything seems to be going wrong.

They know that, whatever appearances are, God is in control of their lives and is doing what is good for them.

With the gifts of the Spirit, it is clear that certain gifts are especially given to certain individuals. With the fruits of the Spirit, however, it is different. These are all characteristics that each of us should display.

According to the Scriptures, there are degrees of fruitfulness. This is due to the fact that fruit does not appear full grown. It comes forth in our lives much as fruit would grow on a fruit tree. It begins small, but it grows daily until, under optimum conditions, it reaches maturity.

The first and greatest of the fruits of the spirit is love. If we have no love, the Scriptures clearly teach us, we are *"worth nothing at all"* (1 Corinthians 13: 2, TLB).

The are several different words translated into English as *love*. One of them is *eros*, "a sensual love." Another is *philio*, "a brotherly or human love." *Agape* was the word translated to mean "divine love, God's love," what the King James Version of the Bible calls *charity*. This is the love that we want to see continually nurtured in our lives. God's love is "a strong, intense, tender compassionate devotion and dedication to the well-being of another person."

The first two commandments God has given us are to love: the first, to love Him, and the second, to share His love with those around us. When we love, He said, we are fulfilling all of the law.

Love is more than words. It produces action, causing us to do something for the person we love. Because God loved us, He sent Jesus to die for us. During His time on the Earth, Jesus was much more than a teacher. He was a man of deeds, and those deeds were the expression of His love. Love had its perfect expression among men in the Lord Jesus Christ. When we love, we must also do good to those around us.

Because God loves us, He *"chastens"* us (Hebrews 12:6) or *"disciplines"* us (Revelation 3:19, TLB). When we love, we will do whatever is necessary to bless our brothers, even if they resent it and misunderstand our motives at times.

Love took Jesus to the cross, and for the joy set before Him, He was able to endure the cross. Now His love in us will take us wherever we need to be and His joy will cause us to do whatever we need to do to express God's love to the world. The price He paid to express His love to us causes us to be willing to pay any price to express His love to others.

In love, we are to *"serve one another"* (Galatians 5:13). If necessary, we are to lay down our lives for each other (see 1 John 3:16).

God's love is infinite, and it is awesome. Learn to express it to the world.

When God's love is not in us, it indicates that we are not fully immersed in Him. We are not *"born of God"*:

> *Beloved, let us love one another: for love is of God; and every one that loveth is born of God and knoweth God. He that loveth not knoweth not God; for God is love.* 1 John 4:7-8

God's love in us is the greatest indicator to the world that we are His:

> *By this shall all man know that ye are My disciples, if ye have love one to another.*
> John 13:35

God's love in us also speaks to our own hearts, confirming to us that we are *"passed from death unto life"*:

> *We know that we have passed from death unto life, because we love the brethren. He that loveth not his brother abideth in death.*
> 1 John 3:14

God's love is not to be found in the world or in the worldly. The love of the world is selfish and fickle. This so-called love leads men and women into serious sin and often destroys their lives. God's love redeems and lifts us to greatness.

So what does the fruit of love have to do with laughter? Those who genuinely love are the happiest people in the world. Even when God's people make what the world would consider to be "great sacrifice," it brings them great joy. Loving people are laughing people.

SEVEN

JOY AND LAUGHTER

But the fruit of the Spirit is ... JOY ... .
Galatians 5:22

The connection between laughter and joy, as I said earlier, is obvious. This fruit produces the fountain of mirth we feel when we laugh in the Spirit.

The Greek word translated *joy* is *chara* and denotes "an emotional excitement." In case you haven't heard, God is emotional. He gets excited. He becomes glad. He gets delighted. Our God is very emotionally expressive, and we are created in His image.

Some see God as a sober judge sitting on a throne with a stern look on His face, ready to judge the world and bring everybody into damnation. Some see Him as a hard taskmaster, ready to bring us all into subjection. This is not a proper picture of our God. He's not like that. These are misconceptions, and we need to get our thinking straightened out so that we can know and understand who God really is and what He is really like.

God is a God of joy. His joy that has been given to us can be defined as: "a state of well being, of gladness and delighting and assurance that is based on our inner awareness of God and His faithfulness."

The Scriptures call all believers to rejoice in every situation:

> *Wherein ye greatly rejoice, though now for a season, if need be, ye are in heaviness through manifold temptations:* 1 Peter 1:6

> *Rejoice in the Lord alway: and again I say, Rejoice.* Philippians 4:4

> *Rejoice evermore.* 1 Thessalonians 5:16

Jesus was our example. He maintained His joy in the midst of the suffering and shame of the cross. It was the joy, in fact, that enabled Him to endure that greatest of trials:

> *Looking unto Jesus the Author and Finisher of our faith; who for the joy that was set before*

Him endured the cross, despising the shame,
and is set down at the right hand of the throne
of God. Hebrews 12:2

If you will get joy set before you, you can endure anything, and you can laugh while you are enduring it for the glory of God. Let the joy that is set before you enable you to witness wherever God places your light in this dark world. Let the joy that is set before you enable you to shine in your work place, in your classroom, in your home, in your grocery store, in your department store, at your gas station or wherever you happen to be at the moment. You will be surprised at the way people will respond to your joy. It's contagious.

Holy joy is oil on the wheels of our Christian experience:

To appoint unto them that mourn in Zion, to
give unto them beauty for ashes, the oil of joy
for mourning, the garment of praise for the
spirit of heaviness; that they might be called
trees of righteousness, the planting of the LORD,
that He might be glorified. Isaiah 61:3

All of us need more joy in our lives. So how do we get it? The Scriptures answer in this way:

TiCKLE ME SiLLY, GOD

Thou wilt show me the path of life: in Thy presence is fulness of joy; at Thy right hand there are pleasures for evermore. Psalm 16:11

Thy words were found, and I did eat them; and thy word was unto me the joy and rejoicing of mine heart. Jeremiah 15:16

These things [the teaching of abiding in the vine] *have I spoken unto you, that My joy might remain in you, and that your joy might be full.* John 15:11

Hitherto have ye asked nothing in My name: ask, and ye shall receive, that your joy may be full. John 16:24

Now the God of hope fill you with all joy and peace in believing, that ye may abound in hope, through the power of the Holy Ghost.
Romans 15:13

Thou hast loved righteousness, and hated iniquity; therefore God, even thy God, hath anointed thee with the oil of gladness above thy fellows.
Hebrews 1:9

The joy which the Lord gives cannot be taken from us:

JOY AND LAUGHTER

And ye now therefore have sorrow: but I will see you again, and your heart shall rejoice, and your joy no man taketh from you.

John 16:22

The verb *taketh* in the King James English (*takes* in our modern vernacular) is in the present perfect tense and shows a continual action. No man can take our joy from us today, and no man can take it from us tomorrow. Like Jesus, our joy was meant to be the same yesterday, the same today and the same tomorrow. Like Jesus, our joy was meant to stay with us forever.

The fact that *taketh* is in the present tense shows us that this is a NOW word. This promise is not just for the past, and not just for the future. It is NOW that God has promised to give us joy that no one can take away from us. And since we are always living in the NOW, this promise is for every day, for ALL of time.

So if no one can take it from us, why is it that we often don't have any joy? Although no one else can take it from us, we often lay it down ourselves. Like many things in the Christian life, it is a choice each of us must make, and I challenge you today to make the decision not to allow anyone or anything to rob you of your joy. You have no greater treasure. Guard it well. Refuse to give it up. Refuse to release it for any reason. Refuse to let it go. Later in the book we will discuss ways to protect your joy. It's worth protecting.

EiGHT

PEACE AND LAUGHTER

But the fruit of the Spirit is ... PEACE ... .
Galatians 5:22

A believer must have peace in order to experience laughter. Peace is the road that laughter rides on. Satan knows that if he can destroy our peace, then we will lose our ability to laugh at his schemes against us.

The Greek word translated here as *peace* is *eirene* and means "a state of quietness, a state of rest, a state of repose, a state of harmony, a state of order, a state of security." In the midst of turmoil, God gives rest and quietness to His children. This is a great miracle, and it creates great joy and rejoicing in all those who experience it.

Whatever you do, don't let the enemy rob you of your peace. Refuse to let it go. He can't take it unless you let him do it. When he brings strife to your life, when he brings people who are carnal minded and walking in the flesh and they attempt to disturb your spirit, refuse to let it happen.

When Satan tries to take my peace, I let him know who's boss. I turn the tables on him and do damage to his kingdom. He has no right to touch my peace, and he'd better not try it. My peace is blood-bought.

God's will is for our peace to be a constant, not something we experience sporadically. He is ready to cause a river of peace to flow through us.

> *O that thou hadst hearkened to My commandments! then had thy peace been as a river, and thy righteousness as waves of the sea.*
> Isaiah 48:18

Peace, as we have seen, is a fruit of the Spirit's presence in our lives. Peace also comes by loving God and His law, by being spiritually minded. Although peace is a promise to all believers, there are many things that can disrupt our peace if we let them. Therefore, maintaining peace requires diligence on our part. To be *diligent* is "to be steady and earnest" and "energetic application of effort." The Scriptures show us:

PEACE AND LAUGHTER

Depart from evil, and do good; seek peace, and pursue it.   Psalm 34:14

Follow peace with all men, and holiness, without which no man shall see the Lord: Looking diligently lest any man fail of the grace of God; lest any root of bitterness springing up trouble you, and thereby many be defiled.

Hebrews 12:14-15

Wherefore, beloved, seeing that ye look for such things, be diligent that ye may be found of Him in peace, without spot, and blameless.

2 Peter 3:14

If having peace requires that we go after it, what are we waiting for? Let us do whatever it takes to live in perfect peace.

God has called us not only to have peace but to be peacemakers:

Blessed are the peacemakers: for they shall be called the children of God.   Matthew 5:9

But the meek shall inherit the earth; and shall delight themselves in the abundance of peace.

Psalm 37:11

Peace is the sign of a *"perfect man"*:

> *Mark the perfect man, and behold the upright:*
> *for the end of that man is peace.*
>
> Psalm 37:37

The peace of God cannot be explained by circumstances or things or by a man's knowledge. Today people want an explanation for everything, but some things simply cannot be explained. The fruit of peace is a gift from God and is unrelated to what we have or who we know.

When He was on Earth, Jesus exhibited complete peace. His very birth pronounced *"on earth peace, good will toward men"* (Luke 2:14). Jesus lived in peace. Not once did He ever exhibit a sense of lack. He never got "uptight" when His ministry had financial needs. He exhibited no sense of guilt at having displeased His Father in some way. He had no fear or anxiety or restlessness, even in the midst of the storms of life. He faced the most difficult circumstances, yet He did it calmly and with confidence.

When He left the Earth, Jesus left peace for those who would love and follow Him:

> *Peace I leave with you, my peace I give unto*

you: not as the world giveth, give I unto you.
Let not your heart be troubled, neither let it be
afraid.   John 14:27

Peaceful people are happy people. They trust God, and they can laugh and enjoy life. When the storms of life rage all around them, they can rest in God's peace and laugh at Satan's feeble attempts to destroy them.

NiNE

LONGSUFFERiNG [PATiENCE]
AND LAUGHTER

*But the fruit of the Spirit is ... LONGSUFFER-
ING ... .*   Galatians 5:22

Patience and laughter work together. Impatient
people find little to laugh about in life. On the other
hand, the ability to laugh at life's circumstances often makes it possible for us to maintain our patience
in times of trial and affliction. Laughter is a reflec-
tion of a right attitude toward affliction. Patience and
laughter: the one feeds the other.

The Greek word translated as *longsuffering* or *patience* is *makrothumia* and means "the possession and
demonstration of endurance while under distress,

characterized by being quiet and uncomplaining, tender but yet forbearing, gentle, unhurried, submissive, and yet persistent." Longsuffering is an important fruit that we all need to believe for.

Our attitude maintained in times of affliction and trial is just as important as the fact that we endure. Every believer needs to have periodic attitude checks. If we endure, but God is not glorified because of the bad attitude we display, something is wrong.

When the Holy Spirit is in control of our lives, supernatural power is released within us which produces the fruit of longsuffering. Many short-circuit the flow of God's power when they become impatient and begin to complain and criticize.

When Paul and Silas were imprisoned in Philippi, they chose to pray and sing praises to God rather than complain and take the woe-is-me attitude. They did not want to become bitter and argue with God, for God was the only one who could set them free. It wasn't long before the foundations of the prison began to shake, the doors came open, their shackles fell off and they were free to go. If they had taken a different attitude and had complained and criticized, the jailer and his family might never have been saved. As it was, the entire family came to Christ when they saw the fruit of longsuffering in the disciples and the miracles it produced.

TICKLE ME SILLY, GOD

God has a purpose for every trial that He allows to come into our lives. He said:

Tribulation worketh patience.   Romans 5:3

For they verily for a few days chastened us after their own pleasure; but He for our profit, that we might be partakers of His holiness.
Hebrews 12:10

Afterward it yieldeth the peaceable fruit of righteousness.   Hebrews 12:11

The trying of your faith worketh patience.
James 1:3

He shall receive the crown of life which the Lord hath promised to them that love Him.
James 1:12

... make you perfect, stablish, strengthen settle you.   1 Peter 5:10

Those who exhibit this gift are happy and gregarious people and can laugh with the joy of the Lord when, all around them, things seem to be going wrong. These people know God, and they know His promises. Therefore, they don't let anything or anyone disturb their spirits. They laugh through every trial.

TEN

FAITH [FAITHFULNESS] AND LAUGHTER

But the fruit of the Spirit is ... FAITH ... .

Galatians 5:22

Often it takes great faith to laugh when those unseen things that God has promised have not yet come to pass. Our laughter, however, shows that we have faith that He will indeed fulfill His promises.

The word that the King James Version translates as *faith* is often translated as faithfulness. Faith produces faithfulness.

Our word *faith* is translated from the Greek word *pistis,* meaning "a firm conviction upon hearing." The Greek derivative *pisteno* means "producing a full acknowledgment of God's revelation or truth." When the Spirit controls our lives, He places within us an abiding and consistent faith that causes us to remain true to God and His Word.

The Scriptures clearly show us that God has given each of us a *"measure of faith"*:

> *God hath dealt to every man the measure of faith.* Romans 12:3

In other words, God has given every man the ability to receive the gifts and graces which He provides. What we do with our faith, however, is the important thing. Can God depend on us to be faithful with what He has given us?

We always think it's a matter of our deciding to trust God, but it is just as much a matter of God being able to trust us. It's not nearly as much about how much faith we have as it is about whether or not we become worthy of that faith, worthy of the confidence God has chosen to place in us. God is ready to answer our prayer, but are we ready to answer His call?

We all know that our faith can grow and that it comes *"by hearing the Word of God"*:

> *Faith cometh by hearing and hearing by the word of God.* Romans 10:17

Many have not realized, however, that faith must

produce, must result in works. The works are the fruit that proves faith's existence. It is your works that prove to God and to others your faithfulness to Him. Much has been written about faith and faithfulness, so let us leave it there.

Those who have the settled assurance that faith brings are happy and joyful people and can laugh when life's storms rage all around them. What could be more important? Faith is such a vast subject that we could say much more here, but there are other important fruits to cover.

ELEVEN

MEEKNESS [HUMILITY]
AND LAUGHTER

But the fruit of the Spirit is ... MEEKNESS .... .
Galatians 5:22-23

It may be more difficult for some to see the connection between meekness and laughter. It is not as obvious as some of the other fruits. God has called us to serve Him and one another willingly and joyfully, and the attitude of the servant is reflected in his ability to laugh.

Meekness is a natural fruit of the Spirit's presence in our lives. The English word *meekness* is translated from the Greek word *praotes* and may be defined as "a disposition of humility before God and man." According to Vine's Expository Dictionary, meekness is "an inwrought grace of the soul and the exercises of it are first and chiefly towards God. It is that temper of the spirit in which we accept His dealings with us as good and therefore without disputing or resisting." It is closely linked with the word *tapeinophrosune* also translated as "humility." Clearly, humility is one of the most important Bible teachings, and every man and woman of God should be clothed in it. A river of humility should be flowing out of each of us.

Meekness involves having a right understanding of ourselves in relation to God. God expects us to be humble and submissive to Him, to recognize Him as the Creator and Giver of all Life, and ourselves as the creature, His loving children.

The Scriptures are abundantly clear on this point:

> *Humble yourselves therefore under the mighty hand of God, that He may exalt you in due time.*
> 1 Peter 5:6

Meek people know that they can do nothing without Christ. That, however, does not prevent them from knowing that they can do *"all things through"* Him:

> *I can do all things through Christ which strengtheneth me.* Philippians 4:13

This may sound like a contradiction to some, but the meek know that the reason they can *"do all things through Christ"* is a matter of His grace, not of their own greatness. Meekness, therefore, is the exact opposite of pride, the opposite of self-will, the opposite of self-sufficiency, all notable traits of the carnal man.

The truth of God's Word keeps us humble:

> *For who maketh thee to differ from another? and what hast thou that thou didst not receive? now if thou didst receive it why does thou glory, as if thou hadst not received it?*
>
> 1 Corinthians 4:7

Meekness, however, is never weakness or cowardice, although many have interpreted it as such. It is true that the meek don't strike back, that they don't feel the need to defend themselves:

> *Dearly beloved, avenge not yourselves, but rather give place unto wrath: for it is written, Vengeance is mine; I will repay, saith the Lord.*
>
> Romans 12:19

Meekness is a demonstration of the greatest kind of strength. Meekness does not mean forfeiting one's dignity. People who are meek can stand tall, with their heads up and not complain in the face of whatever persecution might come their way. This is real dignity. In meekness, we choose to suffer wrong and be deprived of our due because we know that God is on our side, and He will defend us and take our part. We never lose when we trust Him.

We are to *"take wrong"* for Jesus' sake:

> *Now therefore there is utterly a fault among you, because ye go to law one with another. Why do ye not rather take wrong? Why do ye not rather suffer yourselves to be defrauded?*
> 1 Corinthians 6:7

Letting our tempers flare gets us nowhere. Being personally offended and irritated does not glorify our God. Humility must be the part we choose:

> *By humility and the fear of the LORD are riches, and honour, and life.* Proverbs 22:4

Some people are humble before the Lord, but they refuse to be humble before the people around them. Jesus is our example in this regard. He chose to be servant of all, whether they deserved it or not, and He encouraged us to do the same:

> *Jesus knowing that the Father had given all things into his hands, and that He was come*

from God, and went to God; He riseth from sup-
per, and laid aside His garments; and took a
towel, and girded Himself. After that He
poureth water into a basin, and began to wash
the disciples' feet, and to wipe them with the
towel wherewith He was girded. John 13:3-5

And whosoever of you will be the chiefest, shall
be servant of all. Mark 10:44

According to Peter's first letter to the churches,
"God resists the proud":

God resisteth the proud, and giveth grace to the
humble. 1 Peter 5:5

The Pharisees were a good example of this. Jesus,
as kind and gentle as He was, spoke very harshly of
them, calling them *"hypocrites"* (Matthew 22:18),
"blind guides" (Matthew 23:16), and *"fools"* (Matthew
23:17). He condemned their ostentation, their salvation by works, their impenitence and their lack of
loving compassion and a servant's heart. Oh, please
don't let the spirit of Pharisaisim creep into your
heart.

Jesus, as gentle and kind as He was, went into the
Temple and was so disturbed by what He saw that
He began to overturn the tables of the money-

changers and to drive out those who took advantage of His little sheep. This was His house, He said, and they had made it into *"a den of thieves."* What is the condition of your temple today? Is it pleasing to the Lord? Do you have a servant's heart? If not, He may just have to do some housecleaning in your spirit. Jesus Christ came to seek and to save that which was lost, and He is our perfect example of a servant's heart.

Those who are meek are at peace with their world. They are contented people and readily laugh, even in the face of wrong.

TWELVE

TEMPERANCE [SELF-CONTROL] AND LAUGHTER

*But the fruit of the Spirit is ... TEMPER-
ANCE ... .*   Galatians 5:22-23

Temperance is another of the fruits more difficult to connect to laughter for some. Temperate
people are happy people, and they laugh easily.

The word *temperance*, or *self-control*, as many trans-
lations render it, comes from the Greek word *enkrateia*
and means "the state of quality of self control, self re-
straint, or moderation in action, thought, and feeling."
Temperance deals with the whole of our lives. Whereas
some of the other fruits deal primarily with the Spirit,
this fruit includes the physical aspects of our lives as

well. This is important because spirit and body are bound together, and one affects the other.

Paul wrote to the believers in Thessalonica:

> *And the very God of peace sanctify you wholly; and I pray God your whole spirit and soul and body be preserved blameless unto the coming of our Lord Jesus Christ.*
>
> 1 Thessalonians 5:23

The importance of physical temperance is clear from the biblical teaching that our bodies are temples of the Holy Ghost. We are commanded to present ourselves *"wholly"* to God — body, soul and spirit:

> *And thou shall love the Lord thy God with all thy heart, and with all thy soul, and with all thy mind, and with all thy strength: this is the first commandment.*   Mark 12:30

> *I beseech you therefore, brethren, by the mercies of God, that ye present your bodies a living sacrifice, holy, acceptable unto God, which is your reasonable service. And be not conformed to this world: but be ye transformed by the renewing of your mind, that ye may prove what is that good, and acceptable, and perfect, will of God.*   Romans 12:1-2

Meats for the belly, and the belly for meats: but God shall destroy both it and them. Now the body is not for fornication, but for the Lord; and the Lord for the body.   1 Corinthians 6:13

Know ye not that your bodies are the members of Christ? shall I then take the members of Christ, and make them the members of an harlot? God forbid.   1 Corinthians 6:15

For ye are bought with a price: therefore glorify God in your body, and in your spirit, which are God's.   1 Corinthians 6:20

And every man that striveth for the mastery is temperate IN ALL THINGS.
1 Corinthians 9:25

When the children of Israel were passing through the wilderness, they grieved God by their lusts:

But lusted exceedingly in the wilderness, and tempted God in the desert. And He gave them their request; but sent leanness into their soul.
Psalm 106:14-15

Physical excess can lead to spiritual emptiness. It can tie us to the world and make us overly preoccupied with the carnal life. This endangers our spiritual alertness and preparedness.

Jesus said:

> *And take heed to yourselves, lest at any time your hearts be overcharged with surfeiting, and drunkenness, and cares of this life, and so that day come upon you unawares.*   Luke 21:34

The reason God requires temperance on our part is not that He desires to rob us of pleasure; it is so that His life might be made manifest through our mortal flesh. When we indulge in gluttony, the sin of overeating or overdrinking, God is not glorified in us. The Scriptures speak of those *"whose God is their belly."* The end of such people is not to be desired. They are described in the Scriptures as *"enemies of the cross of Christ"*:

> *(For many walk, of whom I have told you often, and now tell you even weeping, that they are the enemies of the cross of Christ: Whose end is destruction, whose God is their belly, and whose glory is in their shame, who mind earthly things.)*   Philippians 3:18-19

When we allow ourselves to be consumed with the sin of *greed*, which can be defined as "excessive or quenchless desire for wealth or gain," it will almost surely hinder our entrance into the Kingdom of God. Jesus said:

> *Then said Jesus unto His disciples, Verily I say unto you, That a rich man shall hardly enter into the kingdom of heaven. And again I say unto you, It is easier for a camel to go through the eye of a needle, than for a rich man to enter into the kingdom of God.* Matthew 19:23-24

Ease in the natural often leads men to forget God:

> *And when thy herds and thy flocks multiply, and thy silver and thy gold is multiplied, and all that thou hast is multiplied; Then thine heart be lifted up, and thou forget the LORD Thy God, which brought thee forth out of the land of Egypt, from the house of bondage;*
> Deuteronomy 8:13-14

This can lead to barrenness of life and unfruitfulness:

> *And the cares of this world, and the deceitfulness of riches, and the lusts of other things entering in, choke the word, and it becometh unfruitful.* Mark 4:19

What is the covetousness that plagues so many? It may be defined as "to strongly, enviously, or hatefully wish for something that belongs to another." Covetousness is a sin, a sin that can destroy the soul. Paul encouraged Timothy to *"be ... content"* with the essentials of life:

> *And having food and raiment let us be therewith content.* 1 Timothy 6:8

Jesus warned us:

> *Take heed, and beware of covetousness: for a man's life consisteth not in the abundance of the things which he possesseth.* Luke 12:15

Some people overwork themselves, and this leads to fatigue and the danger of pride. The Bible warns:

> *It is vain for you to rise up early, to sit up late, to eat the bread of sorrows: for so he giveth his beloved sleep.* Psalm 127:2

Let us be temperate in all things. This brings glory to our God and blessing to our own lives as well.

Temperate people are well-adjusted, balanced and happy people. They feel good about themselves and, therefore, experience joy and laugh.

THIRTEEN

PROTECTING THE FRUITS OF THE SPIRIT IN YOUR LIFE

But the fruit of the Spirit is love, joy, peace,
longsuffering, gentleness, goodness, faith, meek-
ness, temperance: against such there is no law.
                                        Galatians 5:22-23

There are, of course, two of the fruits of the Spirit of which we have not spoken — gentleness and goodness. Just as with the other seven fruits, these are tied directly to our ability to laugh at life's calamities. The more we become like Jesus, the more joyful our lives will become.

Before we leave this subject of the fruits of the Spirit and their relationship to our joy and laughter, let me add that Satan will try anything to destroy these fruits in our lives. He delights in robbing us, therefore, we must stand strong against Him. The Scriptures show us how:

> *Put on the whole armour of God, that ye may be able to stand against the wiles of the devil. For we wrestle not against flesh and blood, but against principalities, against powers, against the rulers of the darkness of this world, against spiritual wickedness in high places. Wherefore take unto you the whole armour of God, that ye may be able to withstand in the evil day, and having done all, to stand. Stand therefore, having your loins gird about with truth, and having on the breastplate of righteousness; And your feet shod with the preparation of the gospel of peace; Above all, taking the shield of faith, wherewith ye shall be able to quench all the fiery darts of the wicked. And take the helmet of salvation, and the sword of the Spirit, which is the word of God: Praying always with all prayer and supplication in the Spirit, and watching thereunto with all perseverance and supplication for all saints.* Ephesians 6:11-18

Personally, I refuse to allow Satan to rob me of my peace and rest. I refuse to allow him to take away my joy, my love, my longsuffering, my gentleness, my goodness and my faith. I refuse to allow him to have my meekness or my temperance. I refuse him in Jesus' name, and you must refuse him too.

Our joy is too valuable to play with, too valuable to risk losing. Nothing could be more important to us. **Lose your joy, and you have lost your strength.** Don't risk that fate. Take your stand and protect the fruits of the Spirit in your life.

It is very important to each of us to understand the armor God has provided for us and to be sure that we are properly equipped in it at all times. This will assure our ability to walk in rejoicing. We cannot concentrate on only one part of the armor and neglect the rest. We must put on *"the whole armour of God."*

When Adam and Eve sinned in the Garden of Eden, all of God's creation came under the curse. Those of us who have accepted Christ as Savior, however, have been redeemed and renewed by the sacrifice of His blood on Calvary. Aside from the power of that blood, God has given us other weapons for spiritual warfare. Among them are the authority of the name of Jesus, the Word of God and praying in the Spirit.

When we allow the Holy Spirit to control our lives, the gifts and fruits of the Spirit will be manifested in us. If we cultivate an intimate relationship with

God through the fellowship of daily prayer and make ourselves obedient to His leading, He will strengthen us.

The work of the Holy Spirit in the Church is not limited to a few manifestations. It is the Spirit that draws new converts to Christ, enables us to solve serious problems and repair breeches within the Body, and this leads to further church growth.

What should our lives be like as Christian believers? Jesus said:

> *And He said unto them, Go ye into all the world, and preach the gospel to every creature. He that believeth and is baptized shall be saved; but he that believeth not shall be damned. And these signs shall follow them that believe ... .*
>
> Mark 16:15-17

There are certain signs that God has ordained which will identify believers. If these signs are not yet following you, ask God to reveal Himself to you in this way. Believe for what His Word promises and begin to receive it. What should you believe for?

> *In My name shall they cast out devils ... .*
>
> Mark 16:17

If you are a believer, then you should have power

over demons in the name of Jesus. Cast them out. He has given you the authority to use His name.

> *They shall speak with new tongues.*
>
> Mark 16:17

If you are a believer, you should be speaking with new tongues. This is what happens when we receive the baptism of the Holy Ghost. It is a gift that opens many other gifts for us, so we need it:

> *They shall take up serpents.* Mark 16:18

Snake bites are very rare occurrences these days, so it is something that most of us never have to worry about. My own feeling is that Jesus was speaking of our ability to defeat the serpent, Satan, through spiritual warfare.

> *If they drink any deadly thing, it shall not hurt them.* Mark 16:18

Poisoning is rare enough in these days that most of us need never fear it happening to us. If you accidentally take something poisonous, believe God for this promised miracle. You have the resurrection power of God within you, and He said that if you accidentally drink something that's deadly, something that is poisonous and would normally kill you, it will not hurt you because you have the power of God within you. The resurrection power of God will protect you. Hallelujah! Glory to God!

> *They shall lay hands on the sick, and they shall recover.*   Mark 16:18

If you are a believer, you have power to lay hands on the sick and see them recover. He didn't say they would necessarily recover instantly, although many do. Recovery is sometimes a process.

After the Lord had given this teaching to His disciples, He went back to Heaven. They went right out and began to put the teaching into practice:

> *So then after the Lord had spoken unto them, He was received up into heaven, and sat on the right hand of God. And they went forth, and preached every where, the Lord working with them, and confirming the word with signs following.*   Mark 16:19-20

So, it is the Lord Himself, working with us, who accomplishes the work. Because of His presence in us and with us, we have power to do signs, wonders and miracles in His name.

The Amplified Bible says it this way:

And these attestings signs will accompany those who believe: in My name they will drive out demons; they will speak in new languages; they will pick up serpents, and (even) if they drink anything deadly, it will not hurt them; they will lay their hands on the sick, and they will get well. Mark 16:17-18, AMP

It just doesn't get any better than that.

To all of these weapons, add the weapon of laughter. It is a potent tool that God has placed in our hands.

Children of God, let us go forth to wield our weapons of warfare mightily in these last days of time, and let the joy and laughter of the Lord be part of your arsenal.

PART III

KEEPING GODLY LAUGHTER WORKING IN YOUR LIFE

FOURTEEN

THE JOY ROBBERS

The joy of the LORD is your strength.
Nehemiah 8:10

If we know that the joy of the Lord is our strength, you can be sure that our enemy knows it too. He will do anything and everything to rob us of the supernatural joy we have received from Heaven and the laughter from our mouths. You must make up you mind not to let a thief come into your house (the temple of the Holy Ghost) and carry your joy and your laughter away through unbelief.

There are many wonderful teachings in the fourth chapter of James that we would do well to heed. This passage reveals to us some of the things that separate us from God's blessing, things that keep us from His joy. If we can guard ourselves against these robber barons, we can keep our joy, and, thus, our strength.

In discussing the cause of quarrels and conflicts, for example, James said:

> *Isn't it because there's a whole army of evil desires within you? You want what you don't have, so you kill to get it. You long for what others have, and can't afford it, so you start a fight to take it away from them.*
>
> James 4:1-2, TLB

The desire for things in us humans is very strong. We may not always kill each other for things, but we are good at doing the same thing with words.

James continued:

> *And yet the reason you don't have what you want is that you don't ask God for it.*
>
> James 4:2, TLB

God must be our Source. He wants all the glory. Let Him be your Supplier. When we rely on anyone or anything else, He is grieved.

Another reason we fail to receive from God is that we have wrong motives:

THE JOY ROBBERS

And even when you do ask, you don't get it because your whole aim is wrong — you want only what will give you pleasure.

James 4:3, TLB

When we ask for something and it doesn't come, we should check our hearts to see if our intentions are pure. When we ask *"amiss,"* God withholds His blessing from us. That doesn't mean that He doesn't love us; exactly the opposite is true. Withholding the blessing is a demonstration of His love, and we must understand it as such. Our loving Father does what is best for each of us.

God is a jealous God, and He wants us to be faithful to Him:

> *You are like an unfaithful wife who loves her husband's enemies. Don't you realize that making friends with God's enemies — the evil pleasures of this world — makes you an enemy of God? I say it again, that if your aim is to enjoy the evil pleasure of the unsaved world, you cannot also be a friend of God. Or what do you think the Scripture means when it says that the Holy Spirit, whom God has placed within us, watches over us with tender jealousy?*

James 4:4-5, TLB

The reason God is a jealous God is because of His great love for us:

> *But He gives us more and more strength to stand against all such evil longings. As the Scripture says, God gives strength to the humble, but He sets Himself against the proud and haughty.* James 4:6, TLB

Again, in this chapter of James, we have the all-important teaching concerning humility.

> *Humble yourselves in the sight of the Lord, and He shall lift you up.* James 4:10

Pride is a very dangerous enemy:

> *Pride goeth before destruction, and an haughty spirit before a fall.* Proverbs 16:18

Haughtiness is defined as "blatantly and disdainfully proud." Putting it all together, The Living Bible expresses it like this:

> *So give yourselves humbly to God. Resist the devil and he will flee from you. And when you draw close to God, God will draw close to you. Wash your hands, you sinners, and let your*

hearts be filled with God alone to make them pure and true to Him. Let there be tears for the wrong things you have done. Let there be sorrow and sincere grief. Let there be sadness instead of laughter, and gloom instead of joy.
James 4:7-9, TLB

The word *humble* can be defined as "not proud or haughty, not arrogant or assertive, reflecting, expressing or offered in a spirit of deference or submission, as 'a humble apology.' " The conclusion of James is:

Then when you realize your worthlessness before the Lord, He will lift you up and encourage and help you.
James 4:10, TLB

James went on:

Don't criticize and speak evil about each other, dear brothers. If you do, you will be fighting against God's law of loving one another, declaring it is wrong. But your job is not to decide whether this law is right or wrong, but to obey it. Only He who made the law can rightly judge among us. He alone decides to save us or destroy. So what right do you have to judge or criticize others?
James 4:11-12, TLB

To criticize can be defined as "to find fault with, point out the faults of." Most of us seem to be masters of criticism. And, whatever you do, don't gossip.

James also goes on to say in verse thirteen,

> *Look here, you people who say, "Today or to-morrow we are going to such and such a town, stay there a year, and open up a profitable business." How do you know what is going to happen tomorrow? For the length of your lives is as uncertain as the morning fog — now you see it; soon it is gone. What you ought to be saying is, "If the Lord wants us to, we shall live and do this or that." Otherwise you will be bragging about your own plans, and such self-confidence never pleases God. Remember, too, that knowing what is right to do and then not doing it is sin.*   James 4:13-17, TLB

We were bought and purchased with a price. We belong to God, and He belongs to us through the blood covenant. Still, we are not to assume anything. We can claim only what God has defined as being ours. We should continually seek to know God's will for our lives so that we can walk in His ways.

This fact troubles many believers. They ask, "How can I know for sure what the will of God is?" Let me give some quick guidelines in this regard:

First, do what you know to do. Our greatest problem is not that we don't know what to do, but that we don't do what we know to do. God's will is clearly expressed in many principles in His Word. We must do what we already know to be His will, being faithful where we are, before we can expect further guidance.

If we have a willingness to do what God has not yet revealed to us, He will indeed show us more. One of the ways God can know that we are willing to do what He has not yet revealed to us, however, is by seeing us doing what we already know to do.

What is God's will, for example, concerning the salvation of man? It is clearly defined in the Scriptures:

> *And this is the will of Him that sent me, that every one which seeth the Son, and believeth on Him, may have everlasting life: and I will raise Him up at the last day.* John 6:40

What could be more clear? Souls! Souls! Souls! With whom have you shared Christ lately?

What is the will of God with relation to men being filled with the Holy Spirit? It is made clear in the Scriptures:

> *And be not drunk with wine, wherein is excess; but be filled with the Spirit.*
>
> Ephesians 5:18

If you are not filled with the Holy Spirit, then you're not fulfilling God's will for your life. He has clearly defined this principle for us in His Word.

One of the questions we wrestle with constantly as believers is whether or not to have fellowship with this one or that one. God has said:

> *Finally, brethren, whatsoever things are true, whatsoever things are honest, whatsoever things are just, whatsoever things are pure, whatsoever things are lovely, whatsoever things are of good report; if there be any virtue, and if there be any praise, think on these things.*
>
> Philippians 4:8

We are to ignore the bad things about our brothers and sisters and love them as part of the family of God. This matter of fellowship is clearly defined in the Scriptures.

Humility is necessary to receive divine guidance because pride sees no need to ask for guidance. Presumption makes up its own mind what it's going to do. It is unduly competent and bold, and then asks God to bless what it has already determined to do. Humility knows its place. Praise God for humility.

One of my favorite biblical prayers is found in the Psalms:

THE JOY ROBBERS

Keep back thy servant also from presumptuous
sins; let them not have dominion over me: then
shall I be upright, and I shall be innocent from
the great transgression.   Psalm 19:13

We must be careful not to presume anything.

When David got presumptuous while he was bringing the Ark of the Covenant back to the city of Jerusalem, God showed him the danger of it by striking dead those who illicitly touched the Ark. We can have the best motives, the very best intentions, but if we have all the wrong methods and timing and the wrong people involved, what we are doing will not be blessed. Be careful to do the will of God in every detail.

God has assured us that He will indeed reveal His will for our lives. But how yielded are you? How submissive are you to the Spirit of God? How well do you know your Lord and Savior, the Lover of your soul, your Beloved? If your personal relationship with Him is not deep enough to enable you to hear His voice, you may well have problems knowing His will. I encourage you to get to know the Lord better.

Many Christians are just slothful about doing God's will, and they need to repent. *Slothfulness* can be defined as: "inclined to sloth, lazy, indolent." If you really don't care all that much whether you know the Lord in His fullness or not, if you really could care less about whether or not you have a good testimony toward the world, if you are not all that concerned whether or not the fruits of the Spirit and the supernatural joy of the Lord are evident in your life, what can God do? If you want to be happy in the Lord "sometime" in the future, God's hands are tied. He is ready to bless you now, if you will seek Him now.

Our faith must be a now faith. Since God Almighty is the beginning and the end, since He is the same yesterday, today and tomorrow, you must believe Him for today, for NOW. Let God be all that He can be in you and through you NOW. Take your rightful place in God's Kingdom NOW. Take your rightful position in the Body of Christ NOW. Let God flow out of your vessel NOW, affecting every person that you come in contact with. If you are not affecting every person that you come in contact with, then you are not all that you can be in the Lord Jesus Christ.

If you are lacking in this regard, let God put a smile on your lips NOW. Let Him fill you with His joy NOW. Let Him tickle you silly NOW. Let Him flood you with such joy that you cannot even comprehend it NOW.

Procrastination has hindered you too long, robbing you of God's best for your life. Put an end to procrastination, child of God. Surrender to the Holy Spirit of God NOW. Let Him express Himself fully through you NOW. Don't hold back any longer. Let God have His way with you. Let Him put His rivers of life within you: rivers of glory, rivers of joy, rivers of laughter, rivers of contentment, rivers of thanksgiving, rivers of worship.

If you will only yield yourself to the Spirit of God today and will present yourself as a living sacrifice to Him, He will purge and cleanse your temple so that you can be a conduit for His rivers of life to the world.

Don't let what others think hold you back any longer. Don't let your own lack of understanding hold you back. Don't stay in that box that has you bound and limited. Don't let denominational considerations hold you back. Let God tear down all those walls. Let Him set you free from all preconceived ideas. Let His Spirit have full expression through your life.

In this way you can defeat every thief of joy and you can experience *"joy unspeakable and full of glory."*

Since **the joy of the Lord is our strength**, and we can do nothing in our own strength, what other choice do we have but to fall upon His mercies?

Another serious joy robber is mentioned by James in an earlier chapter:

TICKLE ME SILLY, GOD

A double minded man is unstable in all his ways.   James 1:8

Double-mindedness is definitely a joy robber. I call a double-minded person one who speaks out of both sides of his mouth. Avoid it at any cost.

Through the grace of God, I have imparted to you through this book what I have experienced, what I have tasted and proved good, what I have found to work effectively. With knowledge comes account-ability. What you do with this knowledge will affect the joy of your salvation for all eternity.

FiFTEEN

A TiME TO WEEP

*Be afflicted, and mourn, and weep: let your
laughter be turned to mourning, and your joy
to heaviness. Humble yourselves in the sight of
the Lord, and He shall lift you up.*

James 4:9-10

Yes, there is a time for weeping. It is a time
for repentance, and the result of repentance is our
being lifted up and being given joy and laughter.
The Living Bible renders this ninth verse like this:

*Let there be tears for the wrong things you have
done. Let there be sorrow and sincere grief. Let
there be sadness instead of laughter, and gloom
instead of joy.* James 4:9, TLB

God calls to repentance all those who do not know Him, those who have strayed from Him and those who have failed Him. The time for weeping should be relatively short and should result in joy and rejoicing:

> *Sorrow is better than laughter, for sadness has a refining influence on us. Yes, a wise man thinks much of death, while the fool thinks of only having a good time now. It is better to be criticized by a wise man than to be praised by a fool! For a fool's compliment is as quickly gone as paper in fire, and it is silly to be impressed by it.* Ecclesiastes 7:3-6, TLB

The King James Version renders the third and sixth verses this way:

> *Sorrow is better than laughter: for by the sadness of the countenance the heart is made better. For as the crackling of thorns under a pot, so is the laughter of the fool: this also is vanity.*
> Ecclesiastes 7:3 and 6

But, believe me, God intends your time of sorrow to be temporary. He has not called His children to sadness and sorrow, but to joy and rejoicing. Let repentance come, let genuine sorrow for sin come, let your heart be contrite and let that genuine contriteness have a *"refining influence"* on your soul. Then quickly move on to God's perfect will for your life — gladness and laughter.

SiXTEEN

TiCKLE ME SiLLY, GOD

Blessed are ye that weep now: for ye shall laugh.
Luke 6:21

God said, *"Ye shall laugh,"* so what are you waiting for? The Living Bible says it this way:

You shall laugh with joy!   Luke 6:21, TLB

We have seen that laughter is biblical, that God laughs, that all of Heaven laughs and that God has ordained that His children laugh. All that remains is for you to start doing it. Let God's laughter pour forth from your belly this day, for He said *"out of your belly shall flow rivers of living waters"* (John 7:38).

I imagine that most of you who are reading this

book would not have gotten this far without a desire for godly laughter in your own life. You would probably like to try it SOMETIME, but today might not seem like the best day to start. Things may not be going very well for you today. But I want to challenge you to laugh anyway. Stir it up and remember that *"a merry heart doest good like a medicine."* Laugh in the face of adversity. There will never be a better day to do it than this day. You can always find something wrong with the day you are currently living in, but because this is a NOW experience, it requires that you do it NOW.

Laughing, being joyful is a decision you must make, and no one else can make it for you. If this still seems ridiculous to you, ask God to help you change your way of thinking. You can help by getting your mind filled with His promises. Read His Word. Know His will for your life, and know that Satan has no right to rob you of anything that God has prepared for His children. You are one of His little ones; He loves you more than you can ever know; He has said that He will fill you with joy and that you will laugh; so start laughing. This is your day to stir it up.

As the Scriptures teach, *"Enter into His gates with thanksgiving and into His courts with praise."* Declare: *"This is the day which the Lord hath made. We will rejoice and be glad in it [TODAY]!"*

TICKLE ME SILLY, GOD

Let your prayer today be, "Lord, tickle me silly," and I promise you He will do it. Our great God will fill you with a joy greater than you have ever imagined possible, splashing over onto the world around you. Yield yourself to the Spirit of God just now, and see what He will do for you. Remember, He pours laughter on the lips of His people.

Don't be afraid. You are about to experience something wonderful, something totally supernatural — godly laughter, laughter in the Spirit, laughter from the heavenlies. Join the angels and the Heavenly Father and laugh at the threats of the evil one. Laugh at the *"puny plans"* of men. Laugh for joy. Laugh because God is laughing. Laugh because He delights in the pleasure of His children. Exercise your faith.

With joy, draw water from the wells of salvation. If you are hungry for it today, you will be filled. That is God's promise.

In closing, let us look at God's Word through Moses and see that joy is a command, not an option. God said:

> *And they* [the curses outlined for disobedience] *shall be upon thee for a sign and for a wonder, and upon thy seed for ever. Because thou servedst not the* Lord *thy God with joyfulness, and with gladness of heart, for the abundance of all things.*
>
> Deuteronomy 28:46-47

Why would God ever declare a curse upon anyone? Because men refuse to serve Him with joyfulness and with gladness of heart. And what will serving Him with joyfulness and gladness of heart lead to? *"For the abundance of all things."* You see, beloved, God has commanded you to be joyful in your service to Him.

Amen!
So be it!

MY PRAYER FOR YOU

Did you know that the greatest miracle of all is eternal salvation? If you would like to experience this free gift from God, please pray this prayer with me out loud:

Father,

Your Word declares that "all have sinned and come short of the glory of God," *that* "the wages of sin is death, but the gift of God is eternal life through Jesus Christ, our Lord," *that if I* "confess with [my] mouth that Jesus is Lord and believe in my heart that God raised Him from the dead," *I will be saved. For it is with my heart that I believe and am justified, and it is with my mouth that I confess and am saved. Lord, I renounce Satan and all his works. His power over me is broken, in Jesus' name. I ask You, Lord Jesus, to baptize me with the Holy Ghost and fire. I surrender all to You. Fill me with Your joy unspeakable and full of glory.*

Amen! and Amen!

Please drop us a note so that we might rejoice with you.   — JMI

The wilderness and the solitary place shall BE GLAD for them; and the desert shall rejoice, and blossom as the rose. It shall blossom abundantly, and REJOICE EVEN WITH JOY AND SINGING: the glory of Lebanon shall be given unto it, the excellency of Carmel and Sharon, they shall see the glory of the Lord, *and the excellency of our God. Strengthen ye the weak hands, and confirm the feeble knees. Say to them that are of a fearful heart, Be strong, fear not: behold, your God will come with vengeance, even God with a recompence; He will come and save you.*

Then the eyes of the blind shall be opened, and the ears of the deaf shall be unstopped. Then shall the lame man leap as an hart, and the tongue of the dumb sing: for in the wilderness shall waters break out, and streams in the desert. And the parched ground shall become a pool, and the thirsty land springs of water: in the habitation of dragons, where each lay, shall be grass with reeds and rushes. And an highway shall be there, and a way, and it shall be called The way of holiness; the unclean shall not pass over it; but it shall be for those: the wayfaring men, though fools, shall not err therein. No lion shall be there, nor any ravenous beast shall go up thereon, it shall not be found there; but the redeemed shall walk there: And the ransomed of the Lord *shall return, and COME TO ZION WITH SONGS AND EVERLASTING JOY UPON THEIR HEADS: THEY SHALL OBTAIN JOY AND GLADNESS, AND SORROW AND SIGHING SHALL FLEE AWAY.*   Isaiah 35:1-10

ABOUT THE AUTHOR

KIM OLDHAM KRAEMER is a Spirit-filled woman of faith, committed and bold in her ministry to deliver God's message to the nations. This has made her a dynamic international speaker. Her ministry is a prophetic servant's mission of love and joy to make ready a people for the coming of the Lord. The Lord has anointed Kim with gifts of prophecy, teaching, healing and deliverance, and many people have been set free and healed in spirit, body and soul through her work. Her ministry to the brokenhearted is tender in love and powerful in word and action.

Kim accepted Christ as her Savior as a young girl and very early recognized that she was being raised up for a special work. She was filled with the Spirit in 1986. God then began to set her forth, grooming and laying the foundations of the ministry she so boldly walks in today. Her husband Ron supports her and stands by her side to further the Gospel of Jesus Christ in the Earth. The two of them are ordained ministers with Christian International.

Ministry address:

Rev. Kim Oldham Kraemer
Joy Prophetic Ministries, Intl.
PO Box 313
Clinton, IN 47842

our website: www.jmiprophet.org
e-mail: kim@jmiprophet.org

For a complete list of tapes and books by Kim Kraemer, to be on her mailing list or to receive her free newsletter "Prophetic News," write this address.